Preceding page: The Roman Forum facing west, towards the capitol. This central public space of the Roman Republic and the the Empire was covered with earth and rubbish in Palladio's time, and known as the *Campo Vaccino*, the cowfield. However, since it became the main meeting place of Rome, probably in the eighth century B.C.E., it was transformed by many additions during which it retained its original function. In the foreground are the surviving columns of the temple of the heavenly twins, Castor and Pollux. In the upper center, the triumphal arch of the Emperor Septimius Severus, which spanned the Via Sacra along which the triumphal general went up to the temple of Jupiter on the Capitoline.

In Palladio's time, it was buried up to the imposts of the smaller arches. The isolated column on the left is in honor of the Byzantine Emperor Phocas and carried a gilt statue of him, now lost.

The Roman Forum facing east. From left to right: the portico of the Temple of Antoninus and Faustina incorporated into the church of S. Lorenzo in Miranda. Some honorific columns and the top of the Colosseum. The seventeenth-century church of Sta Francesca Romana with its much older campanile. In the foreground a fragment of the Basilica Emilia and the flagged surface of the Via Sacra. In the background the reconstructed fragment (in the nineteenth century) of the circular Temple of Vesta, which was one of the holiest shrines of Rome, and next to it, under the brushwood, the remains of the *Regia*, which commemorated the first kings of Rome and which has recently been excavated. Behind the Temple of Vesta was the palatial house of the Vestal Virgins, and further the triumphal arch of the Emperor Titus, built after his capture of Jerusalem, through which the Via Sacra enters the Forum, and which, in Palladio's time, was part of a fortifying wall. The three columns are the same ones as those of the Temple of Castor and Pollux shown on page 1; the pine trees on the far right indicate the slope of the Palatine Hill.

The Pantheon, Rome – a shrine of all the gods – looking towards the altar. This huge circular brick temple was built during the reign of the Emperor Hadrian (76–138) and perhaps designed by that illustrious amateur architect. Encrusted on the interior with colored marbles, the cornice is supported by marble monolithic columns. Unfortunately the tall attic story (of which only a fragment remains) – visible around the two smaller windows on the right – was completely reshaped in the latter eighteenth century.

Overleaf: The Pantheon, Rome. Interior of the dome. The largest mass of cast concrete surviving from antiquity is still a technical and organizational puzzle and was enormously impressive to earlier architects. The exterior was once sheathed in bronze gilt tiles, and the five ranges of twenty-eight coffers (perhaps a reference to the days of the month?) of the dome were embellished with gilt bronze stars. The tiles were removed in 663 by the Byzantine emperor, Constans II.

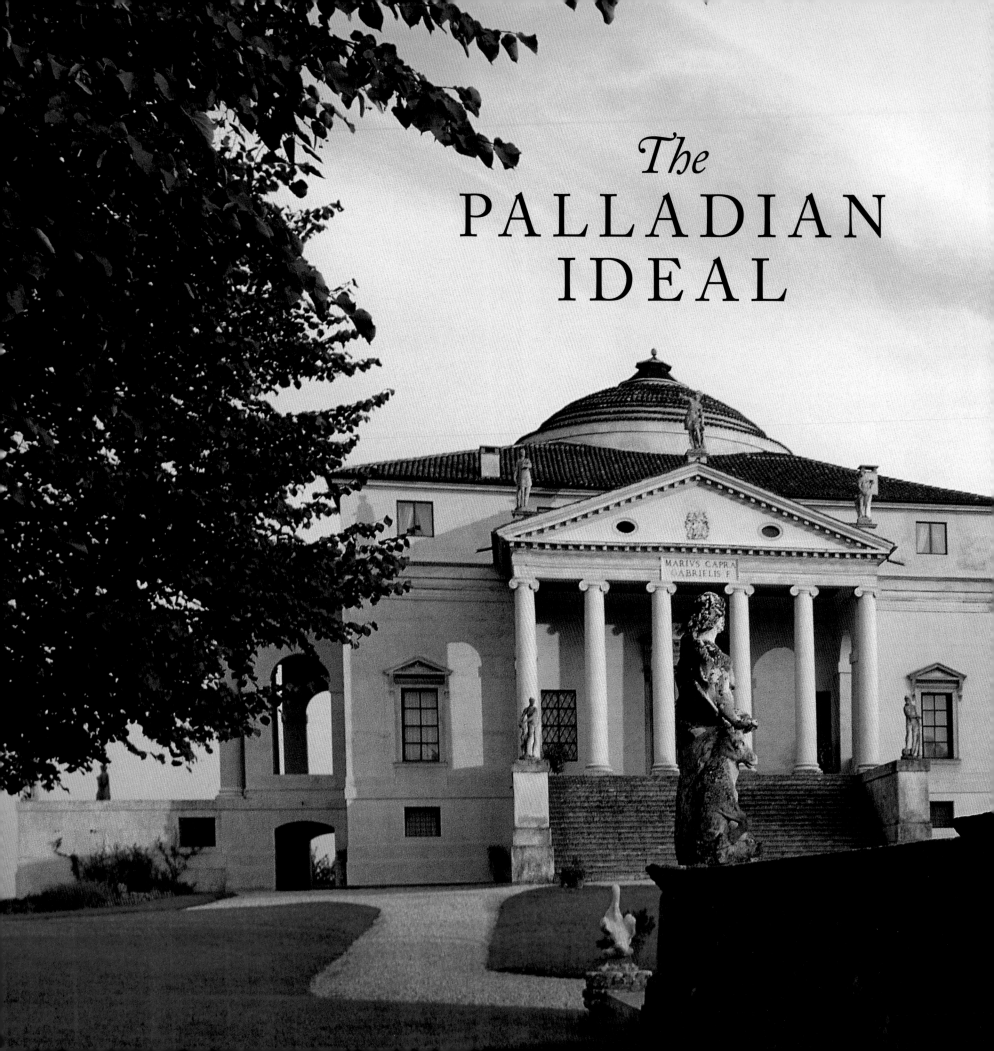

The
PALLADIAN
IDEAL

Text by Joseph Rykwert

Photographs by Roberto Schezen

RIZZOLI
NEW YORK

Acknowledgments

Countess Cornelia Ferri de Lazara
Mrs. Kate Gallop
Mr. and Mrs. Bruce Ginzberg
Mrs. Jane Wallis

—R. S.

First published in the United States of America in 1999 by
Rizzoli International Publications, Inc.
300 Park Avenue South
New York, NY 10010

ISBN 0-8478-2158-7
LC 99-70594

Designed by Marcus Ratliff, Inc.

Distributed by St. Martin's Press

Printed and bound in Italy

Preceding page: Andrea Palladio,
Villa Rotonda, Vicenza.

CONTENTS

Introduction

PALLADIO AND THE PALLADIANS

PALLADIO IS ABOUT the most famous architect who ever lived; the adjective "palladian" derived from his name is so familiar that it may come as a surprise that it was given him as a nickname when he was a young stonemason called Andrea di Pietro, or son of Pietro. His father was known as Pietro dalla Gondola, which was not a surname, but a trade description, suggesting that he may have been a boatman. No other architect, not even his near-contemporary Michelangelo (whom you may well think the greater architect) has been given that mark of glory, even, it has to be said, of affection. Ask anyone and they will tell you what "Palladian" means: a columned building, something harmonious, easy on the eye; in English it has become almost synonymous with "classical."

Palladio's own origin was humble. He was born in Padua on St Andrew's day, 1508; his father, who was by then working as a miller, apprenticed Andrea to a stonemason in his home town. Although little is known about his training, he certainly changed masters and was working for a mason-contractor in Vicenza (some twenty miles away) while still in his teens. The workshop was engaged on a villa at Cricoli, just outside the town, which Giangiorgio Trissino, one of the most brilliant, politically as well as intellectually, figures ever produced by Vicenza, was transforming according to the new taste for the antique. High-born, a friend of the two most formidable women of his time, Lucrezia Borgia and Isabella d'Este, he was made count and knight of the Golden Fleece by the Emperor Charles V. As a man of letters he was an advocate of Tuscan as the literary language of all Italy,

into which he translated Dante's *De vulgari eloquentia* (On eloquence in common speech) In his pseudo-antique tragedy, *Sofonisba*, he also recommended the adoption of certain Greek letters into Italian. The tragedy has been performed rarely, but its original printing by Lodovico Arrighi is one of the most beautiful books of the sixteenth century. Trissino (and some, though not all of his contemporaries) regarded his Homeric epic, *l'Italia liberata dai Goti* (Italy freed from the Goths) as his masterpiece; it was a verse account of the two campaigns that the Byzantine general Belisaurus had fought against the Ostrogoths in sixth-century Italy, though it may owe more to another friend of his, Lodovico Ariosto, than to Homer. An architecturally trained angel, Palladius,[1] guides the heroes at one point through a splendid palace.

It is not clear how Palladius, the angel, came by his name. There were several figures called that in antiquity, of whom the best known was Rutilius Palladius Aemilianus, whose agricultural treatise was translated into Italian in 1514, but the name seems really to associate the angel with Pallas Athena, the goddess of wisdom, wit, and of all craft skills. Trissino bestowed the name of his Vitruvian angel on the personable and brilliant young Andrea, who adopted it, and was signing himself "Andrea Palladio" by about 1540.

The rather dry and scholastic facade of the villa at Cricoli has been attributed to the as yet immature Palladio, but it was probably by Trissino himself. He had some design skill—his architectural projects are neatly and sensibly drawn—and had spent much time and energy on the study of Vitruvius (c. 90–20 B.C.E.) with a view to

Antonio Zucchi, *Andrea Palladio*, engraving after the portrait by his friend Giovanni Battista Maganza, then in the Villa Rotonda, but since lost. From Enea Arnaldi, *Delle Basiliche Antiche, e specialmente quella di Vicenza*. Vicenza, 1767.

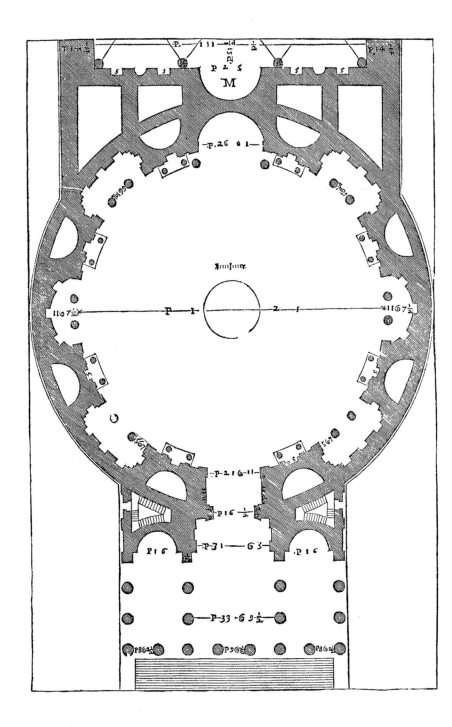

Andrea Palladio. Survey plan
of the Roman Pantheon.
Woodcut from *Quattro Libri*.

producing an architectural treatise, of which only a sketch
survives;[2] it is learning rather than skill that he passed to
Andrea, whom he also included in his entourage when he
made an extensive visit to Rome in 1541 in great state.
Trissino was carried in a litter by two mules; his suite (on
horseback) included other disciples: a young noble, Marco
Thiene (known later for his Calvinist sympathies), and the
dialect poet and painter—Titian's pupil—Giovanni Battista
Maganza (who was probably responsible for the only reliable portrait of Palladio and worked with him on some
projects). There were also cooks, a physician, and a chaplain. It gave Palladio his first view of the imperial ruins,
which he drew indefatigably. He was to make several
other journeys to Rome, including a rather momentous
one in the company of Daniele Barbaro in 1554.

Palladio was to have many connections with the nobility of Vicenza: Chiericati, Piovene, Thiene, Valmarana; and
later of Venice. His closest friends and supporters were
the Barbaro family, who stood very high among Venetian
nobility (even though they never achieved the *Ducato*),
especially the brothers Marcantonio (a procurator of St
Mark) and Daniele (patriarch-elect of Aquilea). Having
studied at the University of Padua, Daniele fell in with the
inspired Venetian triumvirate of Titian, Jacopo Sansovino
(whose best-known work is the Library of St Mark,
opposite the Doge's Palace) and Pietro Aretino (the fear
of whose satirical sonnets kept him in funds from various potentates—hence his sobriquet, "the scourge of
princes"). He had also been ambassador to the cruel teenage
King Edward VI of England, and was named patriarch-
elect by the Venetian senate in 1550, about the time he met
Palladio.[3] At the end of his life he was also made a cardinal.
Although he published a number of learned books, trans-
lations from Greek, and a treatise on perspective, the
translation into Italian of Vitruvius's *De Architectura*, with
commentary, is his most memorable achievement. Palladio
supplied splendid illustrations, and it appeared in 1556, to
be followed in 1567 by an edition of the Latin text with a
commentary; until it was replaced by Claude Perrault's

Andrea Palladio. Survey of the Roman Pantheon. Half-section facing the altar. Woodcut from *Quattro Libri*. Note the intact upper story.

Andrea Palladio, Villa Rotonda
(Almerico-Capra), Vicenza.
This survey of the existing
building was published by
Ottavio Bertotti-Scamozzi in
Il Forestiere Istruito di Vicenza,
in 1761.

Elevation, Plan

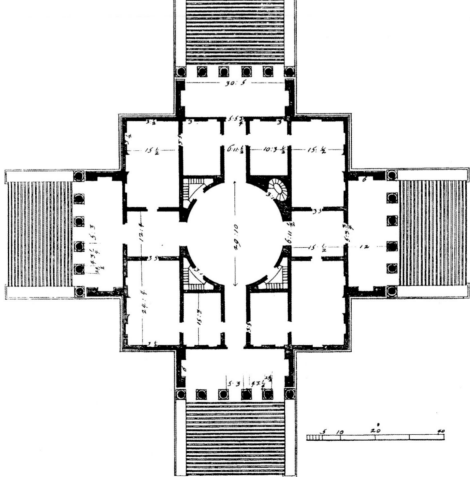

French version more than a century later, it was generally acknowledged to be the most learned and reliable edition of the only ancient work on architecture.

Daniele's patriarchate was a curious office, since Aquilea had once been an important port, but had been stranded inland by the silting of the coast, and never quite recovered from having been burnt by Attila the Hun. By the sixteenth century it had shrunk to a small village dominated by a vast Romanesque basilica, the patriarch's cathedral. Daniele's and Marcantonio's uncle, Ermolao, a great philologist and the founder of an academy, had been named patriarch by the pope without consulting the Venetian senate—after which he had to live in exile in Rome. The senate was jealous of its control over the appointment. Nevertheless, the Republic did not want a resident high church dignitary interfering with its politics as of right, and the bishop of Venice was kept well away from the center; his cathedral, at the very east end of the city, was a roomy but obscure church, St Pietro in Castello. The highest prelates of the Veneto were marginalized, and St Mark's remained the doge's private chapel until the Republic lost its sovereignty. The patriarch lived in the city as a guest, as it were, not as of right.

The procurators of St. Mark's were the highest officers of the Venetian Republic, just below the doge. Marcantonio, having also served his term as ambassador, took over major responsibility for building—even if he did not always get his way. In 1577, for instance, when the Doge's Palace suffered a bad fire, he and his brother tried to use their influence to get it entirely rebuilt according to Palladio's design; but the Venetians were too conservative, and in this case, it may have been just as well. Much earlier, the two brothers, as so many other Venetian gentlemen were doing about this time, had built themselves a villa at Maser (p. 40), some twenty miles north of Venice. It was not just to serve for a few airy afternoons out of the close Venetian heat, but to be a proper and profitable farming concern. This kind of country house had a central part for the owners, the *casa dominicale,* with side wings called *barchesse* to

house retainers, which also sheltered stabling for cows and horses, granaries, dovecots—all the tackle of country life.

These villas were a function of the new economic situation of Venice: the discovery of America and the circumnavigation of the Cape of Good Hope had had a dampening effect on the main source of Venetian wealth, the Eastern trade. Since the mid-fourteenth century, Venice had been expanding on the mainland and its patricians acquiring land there. The papacy, which had bordering lands, the Holy Roman Empire, France and Spain formed a league at Cambrai to curb Venetian expansion, which was not successful. Two independent city-states, Verona and Padua, were absorbed into Venice, though this growth was symptomatic of the transformation of Italian states which contributed to the calming of small-scale warfare as well as of banditism. Country houses did not need to be fortified as they once were, and the Venetian gentry, who had entirely depended on trade, were now looking for new sources of wealth. The estate worked by its lords seemed to provide them with a perfect solution to their economic problems as well as a pattern of rural existence which many of them liked very much. The villa could never be its owner's principal residence however, since his prestige depended on the position he occupied in his home town, and his palace there remained his main outpost. Because his economic status depended increasingly on his agricultural earnings, the owner's presence during harvests and other times on the farmer's calendar—as well as in the hunting season—made the secondary residence also essential. Palladio's invention of the villa as a building type was therefore providential. Such villas, of which he designed about forty (though he built fewer), are perhaps Palladio's greatest invention. It is impossible to select one as typical, since he would play with a plan type and modify its treatment in two or three projects, only to move on to a different organization.

Unique among the villas is the Almerico (now Capra— but known as Rotonda, p. 74) in the Colli Berici outside Vicenza, which took a long time to build, and which

LANTICHITA
DI ROMA
DI M. ANDREA PALLADIO.

RACOLTA BREVEMENTE
da gli Auttori Antichi , & Moderni.
Nouamente posta in Luce.

Con gratia & Preuilegio per anni diece

IN ROMA
Appresso Vincenzo Lucrino.
1554.

Andrea Palladio. *Guide to the Antiquities of Rome*. Title page of the Roman edition, 1554.

Andrea Palladio. *Guide to the Antiquities of Rome*. Title page of the Venetian edition, 1554.

LANTICHITA
DI ROMA
DI M. ANDREA PALLADIO.

RACCOLTA BREVEMENTE
da gli Auttori Antichi , & Moderni.
Nouamente posta in Luce.

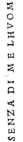

IN VENETIA.

Scamozzi completed after Palladio's death. Square in plan, with an Ionic portico on each side, the Rotonda is organized around a central cylindrical room crowned by a dome. It stands on the crest of a hill and was designed for a great prelate's leisure excursions, for looking down at the town and the fireworks which would be exploded on the surrounding hills. When Palladio came to give an exposition of his theories, *Architecture, Divided into Four Books* became the most important source book of his ideas. *Quattro Libri*, the *Four Books*, has become its short title. In the first of them, he deals with materials and elements; in the second with ancient and modern houses; in the third with public buildings, and the fourth with temples; the houses are divided into town and country ones. The *Four Books* were first published in 1570, though the manuscript had been ready for some time; a fifth book was sketched out and announced but never appeared. Palladio's book is always compared to Sebastiano Serlio's (which was to have ten books, like the ancient one of Vitruvius and the "modern" one of 1485 of Leon Battista Alberti), but it is coarser, less coherent and not as learned as Palladio's.

The Rotonda was included with Vicenza townhouses, not with the villas, which were the glorified farmhouses I described. Although both blighted and exceptional, it has become the exemplar of Palladian architecture. Scamozzi, who had been accessory to the blighting, was the first of many who emulated it, most obviously at the Rocca Pisani in Lonigo (p. 106). In England later, Lord Burlington at Chiswick (p. 186) was to interpret it through Scamozzi, while Colen Campbell at Mereworth (p. 198) went back to Palladio's project as it was published in the *Four Books*, though adapted to the northern climate. And it had many admirers in America: Jefferson's Monticello is the most famous of its transatlantic progeny. The Rotunda at his other famous work, the University of Virginia, is shown here (p. 222).

By the time he met the Barbaro brothers, about 1550, Palladio (who was a few years their senior), was already a person of authority and ready to succeed Sansovino as the dominant architect in Venetian territories. His patrons and clients were the great patricians of Venice and the Veneto: Cornaro, Emo, Foscari, Pisani, Sarego, Thiene. Palladio's enormous talent as well as his learning (which was generally acknowledged) raised him into a social position that owed nothing to birth, or, for that matter, his fortune: he seems never to have become a rich man. "Barba Andrea, what he earned, he spent" wrote the painter Giovanni Battista Maganza about him affectionately. The scholarship became evident in 1554 when he published his guide to Roman antiquities, which appeared both in Venice and in Rome the year of his visit there with Barbaro. Much later, his translation of Caesar's *Commentaries* with many engravings, which he did with two of his sons, was much esteemed, and in fact the illustrations were copied ("from the Designs of the famous Palladio") for an English translation in 1705.

By then Palladio's name was great in Britain, the country which saw the first attempt at a Palladian revival. This was not altogether surprising. There was affinity between the two island powers. The Venetians remembered Britain abstaining from the league of Cambrai. Venetian opposition to the Papacy, whatever its motives, seemed very interesting in a reformed (if ambiguously Protestant) Britain, which for various commercial as well as political reasons, maintained its first salaried (if irregularly paid) permanent ambassador to the Republic, Sir Henry Wotton, a Royal favorite, who was fluent in Italian.

The revival was very much a court affair. It coincided with the reigns of James I and his son, Charles I. The man who was considered its master was no magnate, but a painter-architect, Inigo Jones, born in London of Welsh parents and trained as a carpenter. Not much is known about his early years, though he seems to have traveled a lot: in Scandinavia, in France and probably in Italy. By his early thirties, he was considered a complete artist. Anne of Denmark, James I's Queen, launched him on his enormously prolific career as an Italianate stage designer, though he was really to flourish in the reign of her son,

Andrea Palladio. *I Quattro Libri.* Woodcut title-page of the first Venetian edition of 1570.

Andrea Palladio. The translation of *Julius Caesar's Commentaries* of 1575.

Charles I. He was recruited into the government building agency, the King's Works, when he was just forty, and then spent the next two years travelling—first in France, then mostly in Italy, going as far south as Naples—with the Earl of Arundel, the most cultivated of English collectors and patrons. On their way back, both men stopped in Venice. Venetian architecture, which had lagged behind Florence and Rome, had reached a high point, and Palladio was its most glorious representative. The two churches he had designed—San Giorgio Maggiore, which dominated the view from Piazza San Marco, and the Redentore on the Giudecca, which was the focus of a great yearly civic ceremony—as well as the monastery of the Lateran Canons, called the Carità (now much altered and occupied by the Accademia gallery), were the most important recent and prominent Venetian buildings. Jones visited and admired these and many other Palladio buildings; he also bought the treatise, which he carefully annotated, and even used it as his commonplace book.

When Jones and Arundel got to Venice, Wotton presented them to the Doge. Through Wotton, Jones may have met the aged Vincenzo Scamozzi, who was generally regarded as Palladio's heir. He, too, had designed many private houses, had worked on the buildings around Piazza San Marco, and completed one of Palladio's best known works, the Teatro Olimpico. Through Scamozzi (who was old, ill and going blind—he was to die three years later) Arundel and Jones bought a large number of Palladio's drawings.

On his return from the Venetian (and other) embassies Wotton was owed a lot of money by the government and was also out of a job: one had therefore to be found. The provostship of Eton College had fallen vacant. Francis Bacon (by then Viscount St Albans), in some disgrace after admitting to corrupt practices as Lord Chancellor, was the leading candidate. Wotton, although known to be a man of integrity, had no publication to his name. He now quickly put together a slim architectural manual, *The Elements of Architecture*, in which he modestly disclaims any originality since, he "was but a gatherer and disposer of other Men's stuff." The little book, concerned primarily with the building of a country house, claims the authority of Vitruvius, Alberti, Philibert de l'Orme, and, inevitably, Palladio. It got Wotton the Eton job and its graceful, clear prose made it instantly popular, so that it circulated internationally both in English and in a Latin translation. "Well building hath three conditions, commodity, firmness and delight," he asserts at the beginning of his preamble, and immediately acknowledges its source in Vitruvius: "Haec (opera) ita fieri debent ut habeatur ratio, firmitatis, utilitatis, venustatis…." This truism is often quoted, though its antique source is forgotten, perhaps because Wotton's pithy elegance is so attractive. Although the *Elements* had no stylistic impact (the book was never illustrated), it was, in a sense, the bible, or at any rate the missionary tract, of Palladianism.

As for Jones, he inherited the direction of the King's Works on his return. Almost his first major undertaking was the Queen's House in Greenwich, now millennially situated on the meridian. He also became Surveyor to St. Paul's Cathedral, and the tall Corinthian portico which he added to it as part of the recasing of the whole church was considered one of the grandest in all Europe, though it perished in the Great Fire of London. For the Duke of Bedford, he planned the market at Covent Garden with the "barn-like" church of St Paul, which he designed to look like an Etruscan temple. For Philip Herbert, Earl of Pembroke (whose father and uncle were Shakespeare's patrons) he remodeled Wilton House (p. 176), its double-cube room gorgeous with Van Dyck's group of family portraits.

The most momentous of the early commissions was the Banqueting Hall of Whitehall Palace, for which Rubens would paint a splendid ceiling and outside of which Charles I was to be beheaded in 1649. These were emblematic buildings, in which the revival of antique glories would be tokens of a new Stuart dispensation. The Banqueting Hall would also serve Inigo Jones as an exemplar of a new architecture, from which he would develop a scheme for a vast

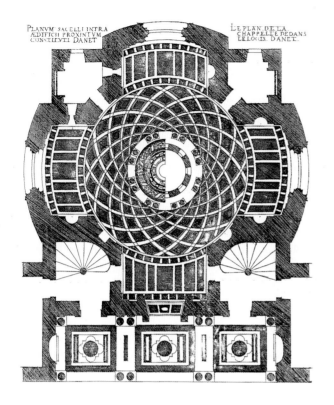

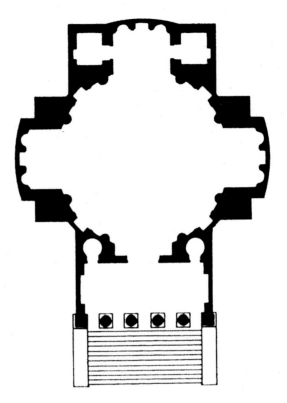

Left: Philibert de l'Orme, Château of Anet, chapel, joined half-plan of the floor and half-plan of the dome.

Right: Andrea Palladio, Villa Barbaro, chapel, plan.

royal palace. Not only was none of it built, but most of the drawings that have survived are by his kinsman, associate and heir, John Webb, who also inherited his collection of Palladio drawings.

Unlike Britain, centralizing seventeenth-century France had no sympathy for the declining and decentralizing (but expanding) Venetian state. Taste may not necessarily follow political alignments, and although Palladio's buildings and his book were known and admired there, his treatise, unlike Alberti's and Serlio's, was not translated. In 1567 there had been a very popular French handbook published on architecture by Philibert de l'Orme, whom Henry II had appointed to succeed Sebastiano Serlio (who had moved to France) as royal architect. De l'Orme also acted for the king's mistress, Diane de Poitiers, and his queen,

Catherine de Médicis. He was a friend of Rabelais with whom he had travelled to Rome, passing through Venice, though he almost certainly never met Palladio, his contemporary. Palladio and Philibert, however, encounter each other in the puzzling—almost exact—coincidence of plan and massing (cruciform buttress-transepts projected out of a domed cylinder) at the Château of Anet (p. 116). which Philibert built before 1550, and in the equally original, small church which Palladio designed for the Barbaro Brothers some twenty years later, long after he had built their villa. Palladio could not have seen the building of Anet, and no engravings of it had been published until after Maser was begun. It seems almost as if, the stylistic differences notwithstanding, the two hit on the same brilliant solution of a formal problem, coincidentally.

In any case, it was not Venice that was to provide the models for French architects, but Rome, with its marvellous treasury of antiquities; what Palladio was for the English, another Italian architect, his exact contemporary, Jacopo Barozzi da Vignola, was for the French, who acknowledged him as the "legislator of architecture."[4] Vignola, who had been trained as a painter, had accompanied Primaticcio to France and worked with him at the palace in Fontainebleau. On his return, he gradually turned to architecture and moved to Rome; there he built the Jesuit "cathedral," the Gesù, the villa of Pope Julius III off the Via Flaminia (known as the Villa Giulia) and the vast pentagonal castle-villa for the Farnese family at Caprarola to the north of Rome. He was, in fact, almost a pensioner of the Farnese clan, much as another contemporary, the Neapolitan, Pirro Ligorio, was allied with the Este family, though he owed his early preferment to his countryman, Pope Paul IV (Carafa), who put him in charge of the fabric of St. Peter's, from which he was dismissed for his rather free treatment of Michelangelo's detail. He was zealously, obstinately devoted to his vision of antiquity and it guided his enthusiastic archeological work as well as his designs. His sometimes rather tortured passion makes his work fascinating, in contrast to the vivacious and seamless vision which is the charm of Palladio's.

The main vehicle of Vignola's worldwide influence was the dry (and somewhat charmless) handbook to the orders of architecture he produced in 1562; it was more precise than Palladio's or Serlio's, since it was printed from copper plates, not wood engravings. In France its currency was such that his name became synonymous with handbooks in general: a *Vignole-de-poche* is any pocket manual.

In England, the advance of a true Palladian architecture was cut off with Charles I's head. The Commonwealth turned to the Low Countries for its models, and the restored Stuarts increasingly to France. The period sometimes labeled English baroque certainly did not follow the Palladian example. When a second Palladian movement began, it had none of the churchy overtones or the court associations of the first one. It was now an affair of the great Whig lords, whose sympathies had little to do with opposition to the papacy, since neither Venice nor the papacy had any more conflicting territorial claims. The appeal was now to a type of constitution in which great landed proprietors controlled an elective monarchy in the name of liberty—a movement of the aristocracy in opposition to the court, almost. "Palladian" finally acquired its English common currency, though it never had the same popularity in French or German, or even Italian. (A floor *alla Palladiana* is a form of crazy-paving, while the English "Palladian window," which has a central arched opening flanked by two lower squared ones, is called a *serliana* in Italian, after Sebastiano Serlio. Neither of them, as it happens, had devised this type of window, though both used it.) At any rate, the English word seems to have been coined when Alexander Pope, in a "moral epistle" about the use (and abuse) of riches, addressed a warning to his great friend, Richard Boyle, the third Earl of Burlington:

> Yet shall (my Lord), your just, your noble rules
> Fill half the land with Imitating-Fools; …
> Proud to catch cold at a Venetian door;
> Conscious they act a true Palladian part;
> And if they starve, they starve by rules of art.…[5]

Pope rightly foresees that Burlington, who incarnated that second Palladian revival in England, will be followed by a host of imitators who will debase his achievement, as indeed happened.

Lord Burlington inherited his title—with great estates in Yorkshire and Ireland, a large town house in Piccadilly, and a suburban Elizabethan villa at Chiswick—as a child of ten. The Boyles of Cork and Burlington were attached to the Whig cause. When the twenty-two-year-old Burlington took his first, conventional grand tour to France and Italy with a large retinue, his absence coincided with a change-over in Britain. Queen Anne, who was the last of the Stuarts, died in 1714, to be succeeded by

A View of the Rt. Honble. the Earl of BURLINGTON's Houſe at CHISWICK; taken from the Road.

Veüe de la Maiſon du Comte de BURLINGTON, a CHISWICK; (a 5 Miles de Londres) priſe du grand Chemin.

J. Donowell del.
Printed for Carington Bowles, No. 69 in St. Pauls Church Yard, John Bowles — at the Black Horſe in Cornhil, Robt. Sayer at the Golden Buck in Fleet Street, London.

George I, George of Hannover. With the dynastic change came an administrative revolution: the Tory government, led by that learned bibliophile, the Earl of Oxford, was displaced by a Whig one, in which Robert Walpole soon assumed the position of first minister.

That dynastic switch coincided with architectural ferment. Of the three major architects who ran the Office of Works under the last Stuarts, Sir Christopher Wren was then over eighty. He was deprived of his charge at St. Paul's, his masterpiece, and a poetaster appointed in his place to "improve" the building by adding a parapet to the cornice. Nicholas Hawksmoor also found himself out of

public office, and even Sir John Vanburgh, though allied to the Whigs, was not spared. There was no clear succession to these three masters, however, even if the ferment threw up some notable publications. The philosopher-earl, Lord Shaftesbury (whose ancestry was parallel to Burlington's), had damned Wren's architecture, and in particular the spires of the City churches, in a published letter of 1713 to another Whig magnate, Lord Somers. He called for the formation of an academy to raise the level of the arts and of public taste. As if in answer to Shaftesbury's appeal, Palladio's *Four Books on Architecture*, with "improved" illustrations by James Leoni, appeared the next year, as did the

The Earl of Burlington, Chiswick House seen from the road. Engraving by John Donowell (1753).

first volume of a large collection of architectural engravings, *Vitruvius Britannicus*, by a young Scots lawyer with architectural ambitions, Colen Campbell.

Burlington subscribed to all such publications, and when he made his second trip to Italy, he was much more focussed—it was Palladio he really wanted to see. He spent most time in Venice and the Veneto, and he brought back with him a collection of drawings by Palladio, which he had bought from the Bishop of Verona and from the Manin family, who had inherited the Barbaro villa at Maser. But his prize import from Italy was a young Yorkshireman, William Kent, who was studying painting in Rome and whom Burlington hoped to advance as the great "history painter" who would revolutionize British art. That expectation was disappointed, yet Kent became a prolific architect and furniture designer, and was recognized by some historians as the "father of modern gardening."[6]

With Colen Campbell, Kent built the prime minister's fine house, Houghton Hall. With Burlington, Kent designed one of the great mansions of the time, Holkham Hall for the Earl of Leicester, which also housed a famous art collection. He transformed the interior of Raynham Hall for Lord Towshend. These two Whig magnates made the primary moves to transform British agriculture by rotating crops, enlarging fields, introducing machinery and experimenting with genetics; all that led to the making of that English landscape over which Kent ruled and (in due course) the romantic artists would paint.

The houses which Kent and Campbell designed were ever more formal and tightly organized as their gardens became more flowing and episodic. The house became a crystalline, sharply outlined and orthogonal object in an apparently continuous landscape, as Wotton had already demanded a century earlier: "…as *Fabricks* should be *regular*, so *Gardens* should be *irregular*, or at least cast into a very wild *Regularity*.…"[7] This tightening geometry, and the almost staccato character of the forms which composed the solid of the building, was taken over and refined further by the architects of the next generations.

Early in the new reign, Burlington had been offered a number of state offices—he was also made a Knight of the Garter—yet he withdrew from public office when he opposed Walpole over a tax measure in 1733, though gossip about the true motive was conflicting. At any rate, he remained one of the most powerful patrons of the arts of poetry and music as well as architecture. Handel was his pensioner for a while, and he supported an Italian opera company. Yet his concern with architecture remained vivid. He became critical of the early edition of Palladio (with the figures "improved" by James Leoni) and sponsored a rival translation by his protegé, Isaac Ware. Having put together Palladio's drawings of the Roman imperial baths, he published very fine engravings of them in 1730. Another great Whig magnate, Henry Herbert, Earl of Pembroke, grandson of Inigo Jones's patron, also became a faithful Palladian—and although no drawings by him survive, he is credited with a number of buildings, of which the most elegant perhaps is the bridge in the gardens of Wilton (p. 178).

Still, not all his equals approved of this architectural enthusiasm: that most articulate arch-snob, Lord Chesterfield (another Whig and a kinsman of Burlington), found the concern with architecture exaggerated and advised his son, Philip Stanhope, that "You may soon be acquainted with the considerable part of civil architecture; and for the minute and mechanical parts of it, leave them to masons, bricklayers and Lord Burlington; who has, to a certain degree lessened himself, by knowing them too well.…"

The snobby objections to Burlington involving himself with craftsmen and the business of the building site echoes earlier jibes at Inigo Jones: the English followers of Palladio were, in that if not in anything else, faithful to their master's teaching. However rarified the theoretical speculation, it must be carried through materiality and incarnated by craftsmen manipulating the stuff of building.

All subsequent British architecture was marked by the publications which Burlington sponsored, and by his example. However much the Adam Brothers and Sir John Soane may hark back to the lessons of the Wren generation, it is the geometry and the spare wall surfaces, the vision of antiquity that Palladio had transmitted, which remained a constant inspiration into the nineteenth century. And it was carried abroad: Charles Cameron, Catherine the Great's favorite architect, had been a pupil of Isaac Ware.

In France, although Palladio had been wholly eclipsed by Vignola, a late Palladian revival in the decades before the Revolution was mediated by British influence. It could even be read as a function of that great wave of Anglomania that hit the French like an epidemic about the mid-eighteenth century—and of course the attraction of the clear and sparing geometries went with a passion for what the French called the Anglo-Chinese garden. At the end of the ancien régime, a number of British gardeners were even imported into France, particularly to reform the Royal parks. For Claude-Nicolas Ledoux, who is the greatest architect of this tendency, the publications patronized by Burlington were the most accessible source of Palladio's designs and of his records of antiquity. Inevitably, the Germans followed suit. Jefferson's admiration for Ledoux is well known, and though he had no particular love for the English architecture of his time, he shared the French enthusiasm for the *jardin anglo-chinois* and relied on English architectural publications for lessons and precedent. All this was a prelude to or an ally of neoclassicism, which in turn gave way to a pedantic historicism dominated by archeologists, both of the medievalizing and greekifying kind, that would dominate architecture in the nineteenth century.

Notes

1. Giovan Giorgio Trissino, *Tutte le Opere*. Verona, 1729, vol. I, pp. 44 ff.
2. "L'Architettura: sulla Città." In Lionello Puppi, *Scrittori Vicentini d'Architettura del Secolo XVI*. Vicenza, 1973, pp. 79 ff.
3. The title made him a bishop with the right of succession to the patriarch, but no specific duties.
4. J. C. Quatremère de Quincy, *Histoire de la Vie et des Ouvrages des plus célèbres Architectes*. Paris, 1830, vol. I, p. 335.
5. Alexander Pope, "Epistle IV," to Richard Boyle, Earl of Burlington, from the "Moral Essays," in *Works*. London, 1760, vol. III, pp. 326, 330.
6. Horace Walpole, *Anecdotes of Painting in England* (ed. James Dallaway). London, 1828, vol. IV, p. 223.
7. Sir Henry Wotton, *Reliquiae Wottoniane*. London, 1685, p. 64.

Villa Emo

Fanzolo

ANDREA PALLADIO's Villa Emo at Fanzolo, built after 1561, is one of the most straightforward statements of the villa-with-*barchesse* farmbuildings theme. Each of the plainly-arched *barchesse* ends in a dovecote—a device to counterpoise the dominance of the center and give terminal elements to the lower farm buildings. The lordly house is raised on a heavily-molded base, but the entrance porch is Roman Doric, about the simplest of the orders. The windows are cut directly into the wall, without any moldings or surrounds This is also one of the few buildings where the design and the dimensions reproduced in the engraving of the *Quattro Libri* are closely followed.

Leonardo Emo inherited the estate as a child from an uncle, who was the first of the family to make a large investment in *terra ferma* land and profit considerably by farming it; and it has remained in the family ever since, which is perhaps why it has survived so well—and that includes the cycle of frescoes.

The main entry, with its equestrian ramp. In the pediment, the victory figures in high relief, probably by Alessandro Vittoria, hold the arms of the Emo family.

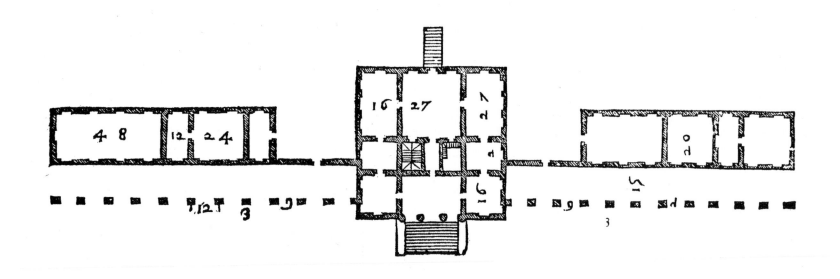

Plan and elevation from
Quattro Libri.

Detail of the vault in the
sala: vine-swathed pergola
(facing page).

Giambattista Zelotti. Detail of
painting in the *sala* (above).

Giambattista Zelotti.
Frescoed wall in the *sala* (right).
The central panel shows the
continence of Scipio, the side
panels a personification of
Venice and Poseidon.

Giambattista Zelotti. Details of a
painted architecture.

Giambattista Zelotti. Details of fresco decoration: Venus and Adonis (facing page) and woman playing a lute (left).

Overleaf: Giambattista Zelotti. Detail of fresco: a *putto* in painted architecture.

VILLA BARBARO

Maser

The central section (far right), *barchessa* and the dovecote with sundial.

Overleaf: The main front. In the pediment, victory figures sustain a double-headed eagle impaled with the Barbaro arms. The dovecotes, fronted by a sun and a moondial, may suggest the residence of the two brothers in the villa.

PALLADIO DESIGNED Villa Barbaro at Maser perhaps before 1557. This is the first important commission that he undertook for Marcantonio and Daniele, the powerful Barbaro brothers. Although the exact date when construction started is not known, 1556 is possible, though by 1558 there were already some buildings on the site. It stands at the edge of a stony but wooded hill (used for pasture), against which the semicircular nymphaeum is outlined, which is watered by a descending stream. The windows of the upper floor are level with the nymphaeum, while the lower floor opens to the main entrance and the fertile plains—the farmland from which the brothers drew much of their income.

Daniele was at the time often in attendance at the Council of Trent (which sat, with several interruptions, from 1545 until 1563), some fifty miles north. But he also travelled to Rome with Palladio in 1554. On that visit he almost certainly saw the villa of Cardinal Ippolito d'Este at Tivoli which had been revamped by Pirro Ligorio and where "nature had been vanquished by art" (as Daniele writes to the Cardinal, in dedicating his *Vitruvius*). Certainly, much of the ornament of the villa—its elaborate and somewhat etiolated stucco decorations—looks more Roman than Venetian. It has never been securely attributed, though it is well known that Marcantonio was a skillful (if amateur) modeller and it has therefore been suggested that he evolved the idiosyncratic style, perhaps collaborating with another sculptor with whom Palladio worked, Alessandro Vittoria.

There is no doubt (though some critics have thought otherwise in the past) that in the main the design is Palladio's, and that he remained in close and familiar relation with the brothers. He published it as his own in the *Quattro Libri*, and the Barbaros were both about at the time. The suggestion that there was some dissension between patron and architect (marked by differences between the executed and the published design, such as the large central window, which breaks the main cornice) also seems arbitrary in view of the later history of their relationship. The chapel was in fact added beside the Villa much later, after Daniele's death. Again, Vittoria worked on the stuccoes, and another sculptor, Orazio Marinelli, provided the statuary. It is curious that Palladio, who sometimes mentions the painters who provided the interior frescoes, does not mention the elaborate interior decorations by Paolo Veronese.

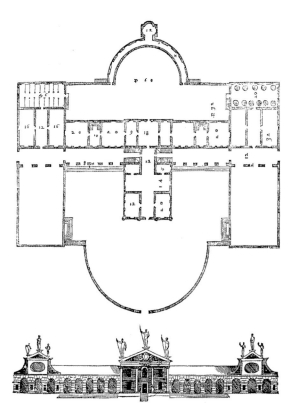

A view, from the house, of the front approach.

Plan and elevation, woodcut in the *Quattro Libri*. Note the discrepancies from the executed design: the more prominent dovecotes, the much more important central window of the frontispiece. However, the plan, including the nymphaeum, is quite clear.

Overleaf: The nymphaeum. The hemicyclical basin and cascade were part of Palladio's original project. The complicated imagery has been attributed to Marcantonio Barbaro, and the sculptures may well have been the work of Alessandro Vittoria and his studio. The fountain is connected to fishponds and to irrigation canals.

Paolo Veronese's fresco decoration of the main cruciform *sala*: painted architecture framing landscapes; two slaves over the door, framing an allegorical scene (facing page).

Sala dell'Olimpo. The olympian gods in the central panel are framed by musicians and pergole. The architectural surround is partly molded, partly painted (left).

Overleaf: The central *sala*. Painted architecture by Paolo Veronese (with figures of musicians) surrounding molded door-frames, within which figures are shown entering through half-open doors. The ceiling frescoes have not survived.

Veronese's decoration of the main *sala* shows a little girl at the half-open door (right). The Sala dell'Olimpo (facing page) looking into the main *sala*.

VILLA FOSCARI

Malcontenta on the Brenta

PALLADIO's Villa Foscari on the Brenta Canal, at Gambara-Mira, is known as La Malcontenta—the disgruntled—because of a legend that an unfaithful Foscari wife had been exiled there. The house was built for two brothers: Niccolò (who in fact died in 1560) and Alvise Foscari. It is nearest to Venice of all the Palladio villas. It has passed through many vicissitudes, but was recently returned to members of the Foscari family. The main front is on a curve in the canal, with a portico providing for stately entry, and two rather fine lateral stairways. Unfortunately, much of the stucco surface on the columns (as well as much of the mouldings and the balustrades of the stairways) has been stripped, exposing the brick structure. It is surrounded by woods, and there are no *barchesse* in sight; in this villa they are quite far away, because of the layout of the property, giving it the look of a small palace. Some quite solid outbuildings had been added in the seventeenth century, but were destroyed in the nineteenth, returning the villa to its original situation.

The rear or garden elevation is dominated by a tripartite thermal window whose rhythm is taken up by the three windows below. They mark the main hall of the villa in the elevation, further emphasized by the broken pediment: the large window area makes the cruciform central *sala*, frescoed by Gianbattista Zelotti, into a kind of orangery. Other frescoes (by Battista Franco) in one of the side rooms were left incomplete at the painter's death (as Palladio recalls in the *Quattro Libri*).

The main front (right, and overleaf) facing towards the Brenta canal.

The garden front (pages 58, 59) is dominated by a large thermal window and its continuation into a triple lower window, which illuminate the main *sala*.

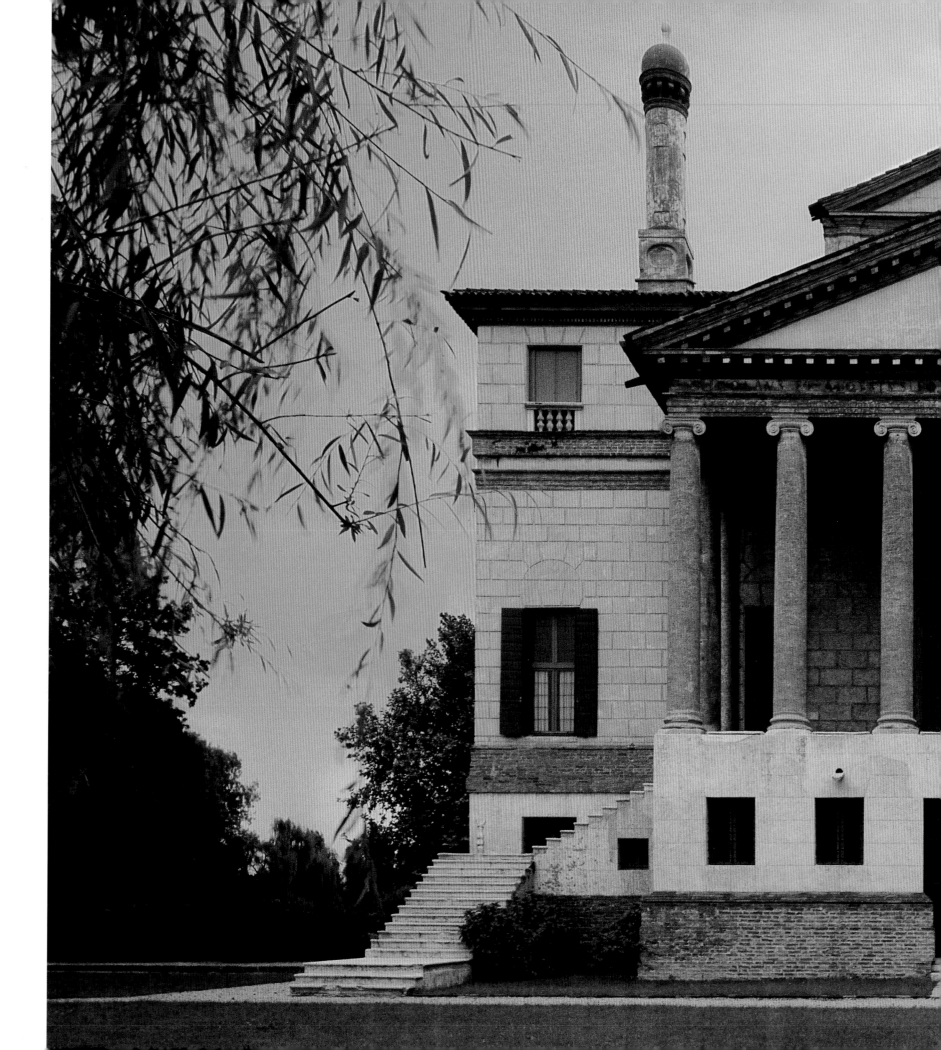

The main cruciform *sala* (facing page) is frescoed by Giambattista Zelotti, as is a bedroom (above) with a pergola motif.

VILLA PISANI

Bagnolo di Lonigo

P ALLADIO DESIGNED Villa Pisani at Bagnolo di Lonigo in 1541–1547 (?) for Giovanni Pisani (also mayor of Vicenza) who bought land (on which the house had burned) confiscated from a nobleman disloyal to Venice in the League of Cambrai conflict, in 1523. The Pisani were energetic and very successful farmers who also carried out ambitious irrigation works. The Venetian Senate recognized their contribution by making them Counts of Bagnolo. The house may well have been designed soon after Palladio's first return from Rome, and even bears a remote resemblance to the Trissino villa, with its colonnaded atrium-entrance squashed between the two (incomplete) towers. This is somewhat deceptive, since Palladio had first wanted the entry to be an apse with a double-hemicycle stair, of the kind Bramante had made popular in the Belvedere courtyard of the Vatican. The rather splendid garden facade, with the thermal window enclosing a free-standing portico, was never finished. It was meant to face into a nearly square, colonnaded courtyard, as is clear from a woodcut in the *Quattro Libri* (p. 66). The barchesse shown there were not added until twenty years later; the design, certainly by Palladio, was altered; lightning struck them in the nineteenth century and they were bombed in World War II, though they have been partially restored.

Overleaf: Garden front, lacking the portico Palladio designed.

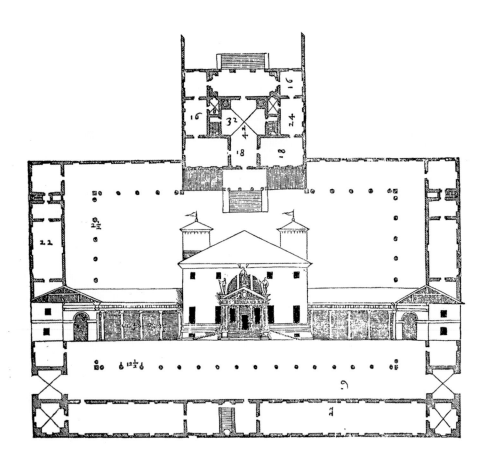

Plan and Elevation, woodcut
from *Quattro Libri* (above).

The main *sala* (right), looking
towards the garden. Although
Palladio's portico is missing,
the three ground-floor windows,
whose arrangement calls for
painted framing, follow his design.

In the one-and-a-half story high *sala* (p. 67), the groined and barrel-vaulted ceiling (pp. 68–73) is frescoed *all'antica* in grotesque motifs and classical allegorical groupings.

VILLA ROTONDA

Vicenza

P ALLADIO'S MOST FAMOUS VILLA, the Villa Almerico/Capra/Valmarana, called Villa Rotonda, was designed after 1550 for Monsignor Paolo Almerico, a Venetian who had been the *Referendario apostolico*, of Pius IV (the official who examines petitions addressed to the Pope). The villa was not finished until after 1600 and until then the central cylindrical *salone* was covered by a flat, boarded roof. The stepped dome may have been finished by Vincenzo Scamozzi. No attempt was ever made to finish the hemispherical dome which appears in the engraving of the *Quattro Libri*.

The Villa was never intended as a place for formal receptions—there are no rooms which could serve as a "presence" chamber—and all doors correspond to window openings. However, it was near enough to Vicenza to be an hour's ride away, and although it had been used on occasions to put up guests, the main purpose of the house was to serve as a background for receptions and parties— the panorama was, after all, its great asset. Set overlooking the valley of a small river, it was therefore not a farmer's home, and such *barchesse* as are now built nearby are later additions.

Scamozzi seems to have been guilty of breaking through the stairways to provide access to the ground floor, and this damage was repaired towards the end of the eighteenth century.

View from west. The statues on the stairways are by Lorenzo Rubini (perhaps before 1570), and over the pediments by Giovanni Battista Albanese, placed in 1606.

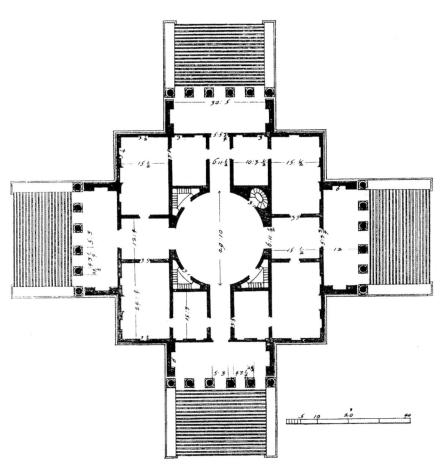

Approach from the south, from
the Villa Valmarana ai Nani.

This survey of the existing
building was published by Ottario
Bertotti-Scamozzi in *Il Forestiere
Istruito di Vicenza* in 1761.

Section, Plan.

Overleaf: General view from the
northwest.

The circular *salone*, frescoed about 1710–1720 by Ludovico Dorigny. The allegorical figures over the front door (before 1600) are by Alessandro Maganza or a follower.

In the dome of the circular *salone*, stucco decorations and frames are by Vigilio Rubini (before 1590). The frescoes are attributed to Alessandro Maganza, son of Giovanni Battista, possibly with his son, also called Giovanni Battista.

VILLA PISANI

Montagnana

THIS VERY IMPOSING palazzo/villa was built by Palladio for Francesco Pisani outside the walled city of Montagnana after 1552. Montagnana is one of the few fully fortified towns remaining in Italy. The castle and the brick town walls were built between 1250 and 1350. By the mid-sixteenth century conditions had changed so much that a number of patrician families were able to build their houses outside the city walls on the mainland, where they were increasingly investing in land, since profits from sea trade were declining; Francesco Pisani was among them and the villa seems to have been finished, in its present state, about 1555, which makes it one of the earliest, if not the earliest, of the palace-villas built by Palladio for a Venetian patrician. It is rather more severe than the similar Cornaro villa at Piombino, which is also an exercise in the two superimposed porticoes formula. Both facades here are Doric and Ionic, while at Villa Cornaro (p. 88) they are Ionic and Corinthian. The street face has relatively small openings, while on the garden facade the superimposed porticoes are open, as verandahs.

This is a small just-out-of-town palace, therefore, rather than a manor commanding agricultural territory, and there are no farm buildings. The plan as shown in the *Quattro Libri* was followed for the central section, though the lateral pavilions which were to be connected to the main part by triumphal arches (perhaps intended to bridge over roadways, though at least one of them would have impinged on city defenses if built as planned) were not completed. The death of Francesco Pisani in 1567 certainly meant that the central building was never extended.

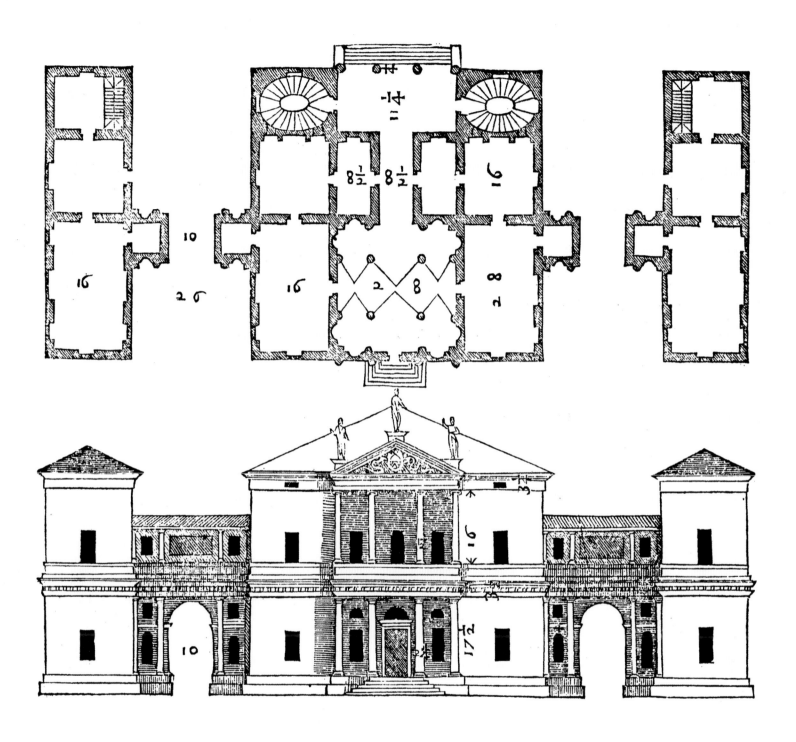

The main entrance hall (facing page) is a vaulted atrium, the vault resting on four Doric columns. It is decorated by statues of the four seasons by Alessandro Vittoria and collaborators; the decorative terracottas in the villa are by a minor sculptor, Andrea del Vento.

Plan and elevation from the *Quattro Libri*.

VILLA CORNARO

Piombino Dese

THE VILLA CORNARO at Piombino Dese, probably of 1551–1554, is one of the villas Palladio designed as a garden-house. It is a village palace with an orchard and a market-garden rather than a farm. It has a double-story portico—a rather Venetian feature—rather like the contemporary Pisani Villa at Montagnana. It was designed for Venetian Admiral Giorgio Cornaro, and building seems to have gone on intermittently for some time. The owner was a kinsman of Caterina Cornaro, Queen of Cyprus, who passed her fairly sumptuous widowhood in nearby Asolo. The statues in the house refer to her and to her husband, Jacques II de Lusignan—effectively the last "Western" King of Cyprus. The Queen, on his death and on that of their son, abdicated in favor of the Venetian Republic. The building is rather more compact than many of the other villas.

North side, facing the public road, showing the Corinthian, upper level of the two-level portico.

Overleaf: Garden front approached by a stepped ramp. At the south side are seen both the lower, Doric, and upper, Corinthian, levels of the double-level portico. Within the main hall is a square "atrium" whose flat roof is also supported on four columns; on either side of the portico are oval staircases.

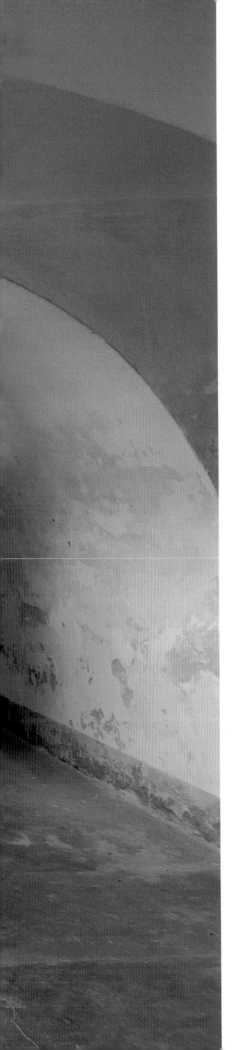

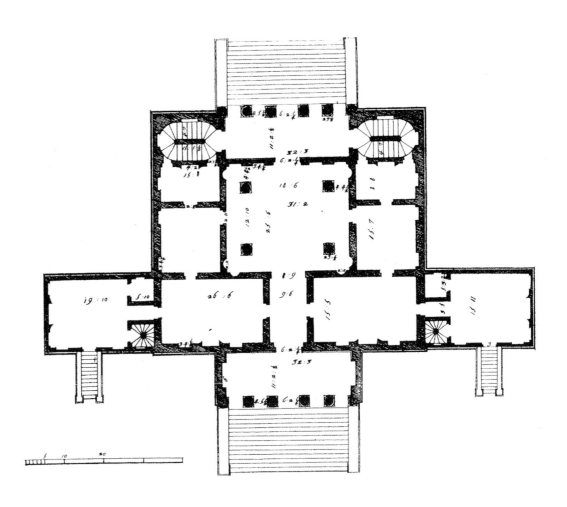

Vaulted undercroft (facing page).

Villa Cornaro, plan (above),
as published by Ottario Bertotti
Scamozzi in *Le fabbriche e i
Desegni di Andrea Palladio*,
in Venice, 1796.

CASINO OF PIUS IV

Rome

THE CASINO OF PIUS IV in the Vatican Gardens in Rome was designed by Pirro Ligorio. Although it was begun in the reign of the Neapolitan Pope Paul IV (Carafa, who died in 1559, and whose tomb Ligorio also designed), Pius IV (of the Milanese branch of the Medici) had it finished and repeatedly inscribed with his name. He installed a great collection of antique sculpture there, which was dispersed by his very austere successor, the sainted Pius V. Not only the buildings but also the very elaborate stucco decorations, both inside and outside, were designed by Pirro Ligorio, who was also a Neapolitan. He had moved to Rome in 1534 and became as famous an antiquarian as he was an architect. He was employed from 1549 to 1555 by Cardinal Ippolito d'Este not only to redesign his villa and gardens at Tivoli (which Palladio probably saw in 1554), but also to supervise the excavations of the Villa of Emperor Hadrian nearby—it was one of the largest and richest imperial sites near Rome. Ligorio was a prolific writer on the antiquities of Rome and entered papal service as an architect in 1558; he assisted Michelangelo at St. Peter's, and on his death in 1564 became its chief architect, with Vignola. However, accusations of malpractice (by another of Michelangelo's assistants, Giacomo della Porta) led to his imprisonment, and in 1568 he left Rome for Ferrara where he entered the service of its duke, Alfonso II d' Este.

The casino is divided into two sectors by a paved oval courtyard, with a black marble fountain for which two *putti* riding dolphins provide spouts. The larger is the casino proper, the smaller is the loggia which fronts the gardens.

The casino, facing the inner court, with the dome of St. Peter's in the background.

The loggia, facing the inner court; in the decorations, designed by Pirro Ligorio, the central shields bear the arms of the Medici, the "palle."

The fountain has by now lost most of the decorations that Pius IV and Ligorio intended for it. The many antiquities were sold or given away by Pius V, and much further stripping was done in succeeding centuries, though the stucco reliefs and the opulent decorative paintings have remained intact. The casino is now the seat of the Papal Academy of Science.

The loggia facing outwards toward the Vatican gardens. Pirro Ligorio's four figures of Pan, which supported the cornice, were removed in 1824, and replaced later by the mosaic panels that appear in the photograph.

Overleaf: The inner courtyard showing the two sets of Ligorio reliefs facing each other. The black marble fountain has dolphins carrying *putti*.

The entrance hall of the casino (facing page) was decorated by Pirro Ligorio and painted by assistants of Federico Zuccari. The statue in the foreground is antique.

Pirro Ligorio and Federico Zuccari decorated the vault of the loggia (left) with scenes from the life of Adonis.

In the entrance hall of the casino the vault (right) is stuccoed to designs by Pirro Ligorio and painted by the assistants of Federico Zuccari.

In the entrance hall of the casino (facing page) the mosaic decorations are by Pirro Ligorio. The statues are antique.

LA ROCCA PISANI

Lonigo

VINCENZO SCAMOZZI designed Villa Pisani at La Rocca, Lonigo in 1576 and later. Although he was trained in Vicenza by his father Giandomenico (who was much closer to Serlio than to Palladio), Vincenzo was radically (though not altogether gratefully) Palladian. In Venice he was regarded as Palladio's successor as the dominant architect of the Republic, and is responsible for the building of the Procuratie Nuove, which completed the facing of St. Mark's Square; but he also travelled a great deal, and was involved in the rebuilding of the Cathedral at Salzburg.

The villa at Lonigo, not far from Vicenza and very close to the other Pisani villa that Palladio had built at Poiana, was designed for Vettor Pisani, an important member of the clan. Although the idea of such a domed villa-temple looking out in all directions clearly owes something to the Villa Rotonda, Scamozzi does not mention it in his account, though he does insist on the fact that when standing at the center, you can look around 360 degrees.

The southern facade of the villa as seen from the river.

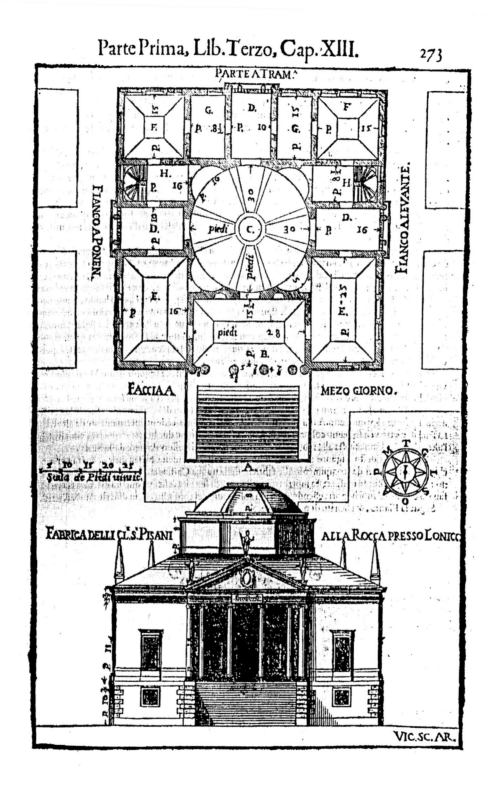

Vincenzo Scamozzi's Villa
Pisani, of 1576 and later,
from a woodcut from his *L'Idea
dell'Architettura* of 1615.

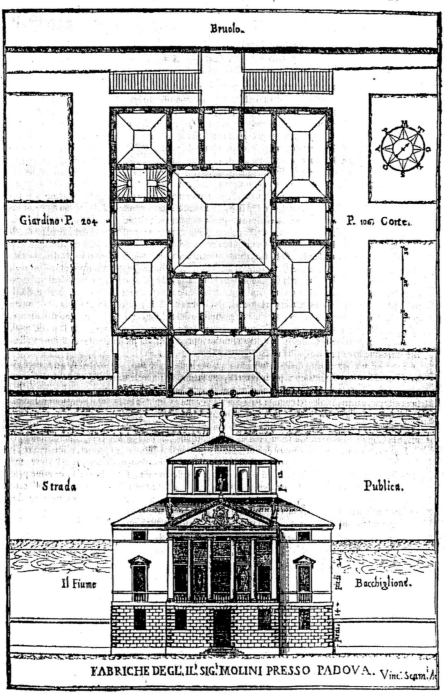

Bruolo.

Giardino P. 204

P. 106 Corte.

Strada

Publica.

Il Fiume

Bacchiglione.

FABRICHE DEGL. IL. SIG. MOLINI PRESSO PADOVA. Vinc. Scam. Ar

Villa Molini, of 1597, in Mandria on the Bacchiglione River, near Padua, from *L'Idea dell'Architettura*. Here, again, as at Villa Pisani, Scamozzi organized tightly compacted masses around a soaring, domed central hall, as Palladio had earlier at Villa Rotonda (p. 74).

Overleaf: The Villa Pisani's main approach from the south.

The interior of the dome (right), and the interior of the domed *sala* (facing page), showing the cut stone ventilating grille in the middle of the floor under the oculus of the dome.

In the undercroft under the *sala*, the pierced stone plate under the dome is seen from below (top right, and facing page).

A semicircular stone stairway in the undercroft leads up to the piano nobile (bottom right).

Château d'Anet

Dreux

DESIGNED BY PHILIBERT DE L'ORME, and others, the Château d'Anet was the castle of Diane de Poitiers, who was the reigning mistress of King Henry II when he came to the throne in 1547. Although ten years older, she inspired his total devotion. She was the widow of Louis de Brézé, *sénéchal* (high bailiff) of Normandy, who had died in 1533 and by whom she had two daughters, and she continued to wear widows' weeds—white and black (they remained her colors)—for the rest of her life. The crescent moon, an attribute of the hunter-goddess Diana, became her crest, and the cipher made up of the king's H and her D appears on anything connected with her. At Anet, which the king gave her (as he gave her the title of duchess and the other splendid chateau, Chenonceaux), she erected a monument in the centerpiece of the building to the memory of Louis de Brézé.

When the King was accidentally killed in a tournament, the queen, Catherine de Médicis, forced Diane to restore the crown jewels (which the king had also given her) and Chenonceaux to the crown, but allowed her to keep Anet, associated as it was with her husband's family, where she went on living, and where she died in 1566. Though celebrated for her beauty in her lifetime, existing portraits show a slightly severe, rather than a classically good-looking, woman.

Many of the main buildings were razed between 1804 and 1811 (by a banker who bought the property), though the destruction was halted by local protest riots. The centerpiece (with the monument to Louis de Brézé) was moved to the courtyard of the École des Beaux-Arts in Paris. Of

The main entrance gate. The relief of a nymph in the arch over the gate is by Benvenuto Cellini. The deer between two dogs (which were in fact a mechanical clock, the deer's hoof striking the hours while the hounds barked) are casts of the originals, now in the Louvre.

Overleaf: General view from the north after Jacques Androuet du Cerceau, *Le Second volume des plus excellents Bastiments de France.* The main gate and the chapel – visible in the engraving as part of the building – have survived on the site. The Diana fountain, (traditionally though not securely) attributed to Jean Goujon, visible in the courtyard on the left, is in the Louvre.

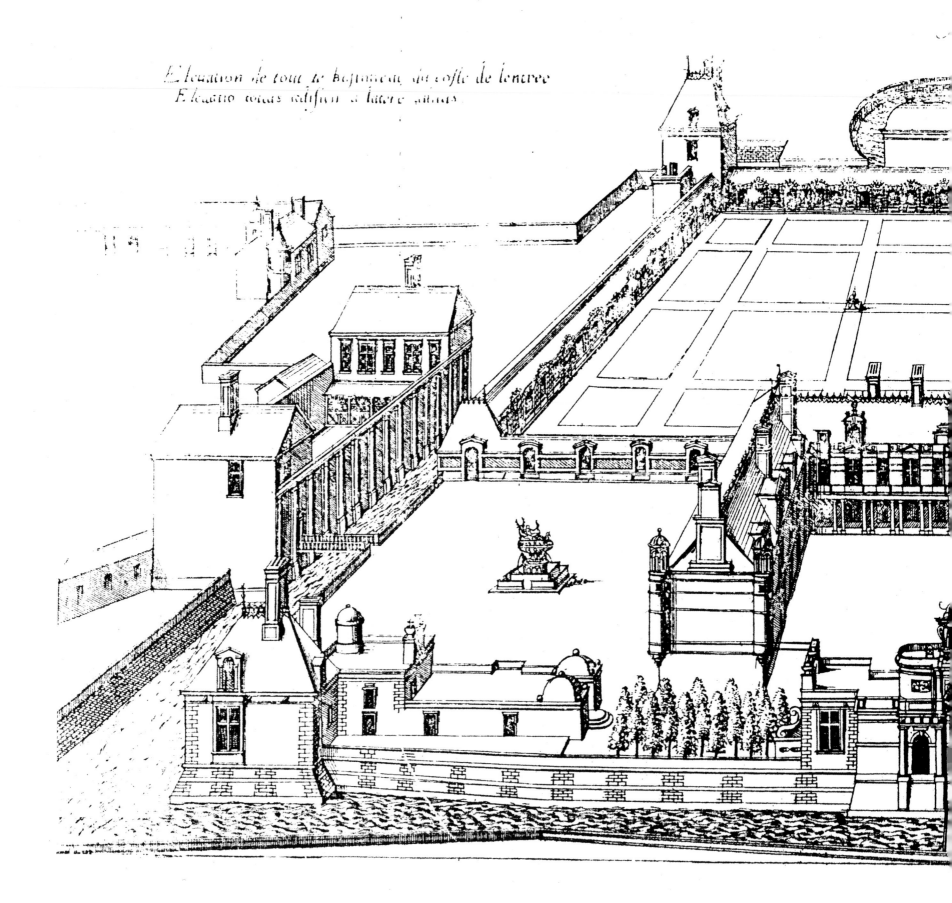

Eleuation de tout le bastiment du costé de lentree
Eleuatio totius ædificii a latere antica

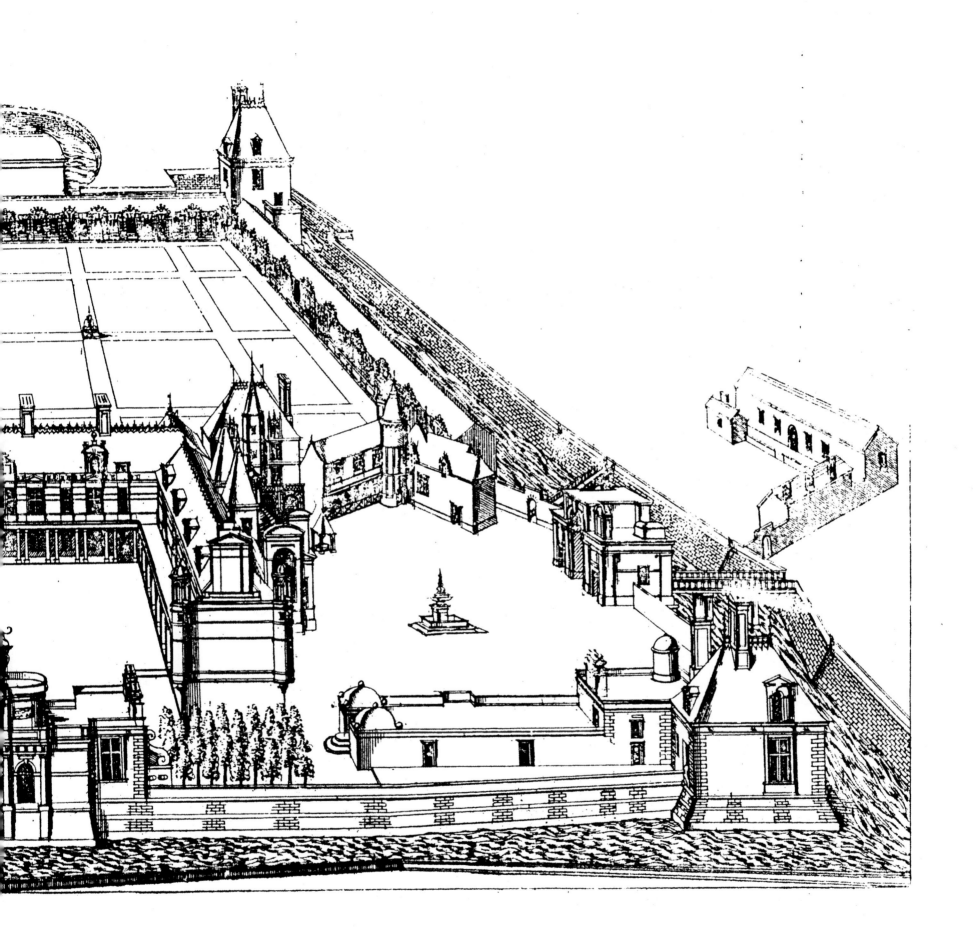

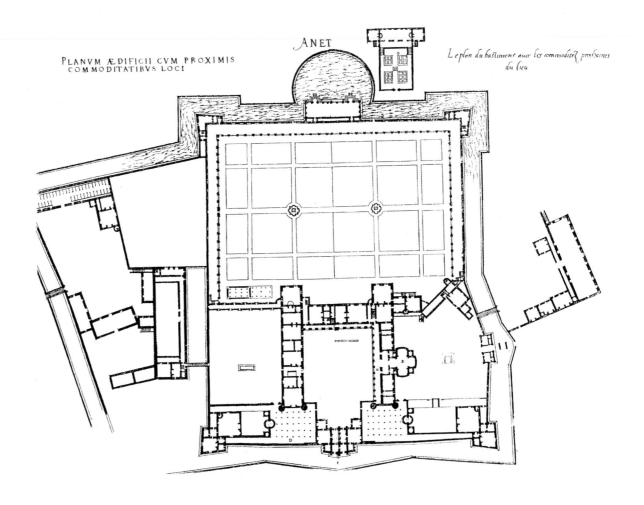

PLANVM ÆDIFICII CVM PROXIMIS
COMMODITATIBVS LOCI

ANET

Le plan du bastiment aux les commoditez prochaines
du lieu

Plan, after Jacques Androuet
du Cerceau.

The west wing (facing page).

Philibert de l'Orme's original scheme, only the main entrance to the château now survives relatively unscathed, as well as the chapel which, in plan and massing, is very like Palladio's little church at Maser (see p. 21). The chapel (pp. 122–128) was designed some thirty years after Anet, and indeed it is possible that Palladio was aware of what Philibert had done there. The building has an idiosyncratic cruciform configuration, each arm of the cross being made up of two short buttressing walls carrying a vault, while the outer walls are curved to echo the curve of the dome. The dome supported by these short arms of the

cross is in turn crowned by a large lantern. The inner surface of the dome is latticed spirally, to provide a coffered surface. The spiral is reflected in the inlaid marble pattern of the floor.

The entrance gateway is a variant on the scheme of the triumphal arch, with three round-headed openings, and four sarcophagi on the side sections which seem to function as chimneys. The rich effect of the exterior is due to the use of different colored marbles: dark grey for the triglyphs, light grey in the superstructure (some bronze garlands over the side doors have now disappeared).

The front of the chapel (facing page). The porch is a later addition.

The rear of the chapel (above), after Philibert de l'Orme.

The chapel. Long Section, after
Philibert de l'Orme

DESINATIO INTERIORIS
FACIEI EIVSDEM SACELLI
D'ANET

DESSEING DV DEDANS
DE LA CHAPPELLE
DANS LE LOGIS

The chapel. Cross Section, after
Philibert de l'Orme.

PLANVM SACELLI INTRA
ÆDIFICII PROXINTVM
CONSTITVTI DANET

LE PLAN DE LA
CHAPPELLE DEDANS
LE LOGIS DANET.

The inlaid pattern of the chapel
floor (facing page) reflects the
coffering of the dome (p. 128).

The chapel's joined half-plan
of the floor and half-plan of the
dome, after Jacques Androuet
du Cerceau. In fact, the two
patterns are not quite as the
diagram suggests.

In the dome of the chapel (facing page) the reliefs are by Jean Goujon.

In the funerary chapel of Diane de Poitiers white marble sphinxes support the black sarcophagus by the sculptor Pierre Bontemps.

The black-and-white tomb of
Diane de Poitiers is in the
funerary chapel, outside the
château enclosure. It was started
after the king's death, and was
probably not designed by
Philibert, but by Jean Bullant
the younger as a much simpler,
barrel-vaulted building.

ABBOT'S PALACE

Royaumont, near Paris

THE PALACE OF THE ABBOT at the Abbey of Royaumont was designed by Louis Le Masson and built, from 1785 to 1789, just before the Revolution by the Abbé Le Cornut de Balivière (not a man conspicuous for his piety though enormously sociable), chaplain to Louis XVI. He was one of a succession of "commendatary" abbots, not the elected leaders of the monastic community but royal appointees, whose chief function was to enjoy the revenues of the abbey. Balivière never occupied the palace, since he went into exile soon after the Revolution broke out.

The gentle rustication, the rhythm of the window openings and the discreet use of sculpture (like the caryatids in the attic) show this engineer taking up the style of his teacher, Claude-Nicolas Ledoux. The thirteenth-century Cistercian abbey church, one of the most important of the order in France, by which the palace stood, was pulled down and its ruin turned into a cotton factory after the Revolution. In the twentieth century the abbey has sheltered a house of studies which has had an important part in the country's intellectual life.

The main approach to the Abbot's Palace (facing page).

Overleaf: An oblique view of the front.

An "Egyptian" candelabrum in the main hall (above).

The open and cantilevered stairway seen from the main hall (facing page).

Looking up the stairway of the main hall.

The stairway looking down into the main hall (facing page).

The entrance from the main hall
(above and facing page).

SALT WORKS

Arc et Senans

CLAUDE-NICOLAS LEDOUX, architect of the Salt Works at Arc et Senans, was appointed to the Royal salt monopoly on the recommendation of the mistress of Louis XV, Mme du Barry. The Salt Works (La Saline), built between 1774 and 1779 not far from Besançon in the Alpine foothills, were the most important buildings Ledoux did for the crown, and one of the crucial and most ambitious ones of its time.

Having been a wonderfully ambitious and prolific designer in the last years of the ancien régime, Ledoux was imprisoned during the Terror and barely escaped execution. Although he returned to his home and office, he spent the last years of his life elaborating the didactic buildings he had begun working on at Arc-et-Senans and producing even more adventurous and extreme projects which were engraved, though many of them were not published, until long after his death. Today the buildings of the Salt Works house congress and exhibition halls for an institution called Center of the Future. In 1983 the Salt Works were declared an historic monument and designated a World Heritage Site by UNESCO.

The director's house with the salt-evaporation sheds on either side.

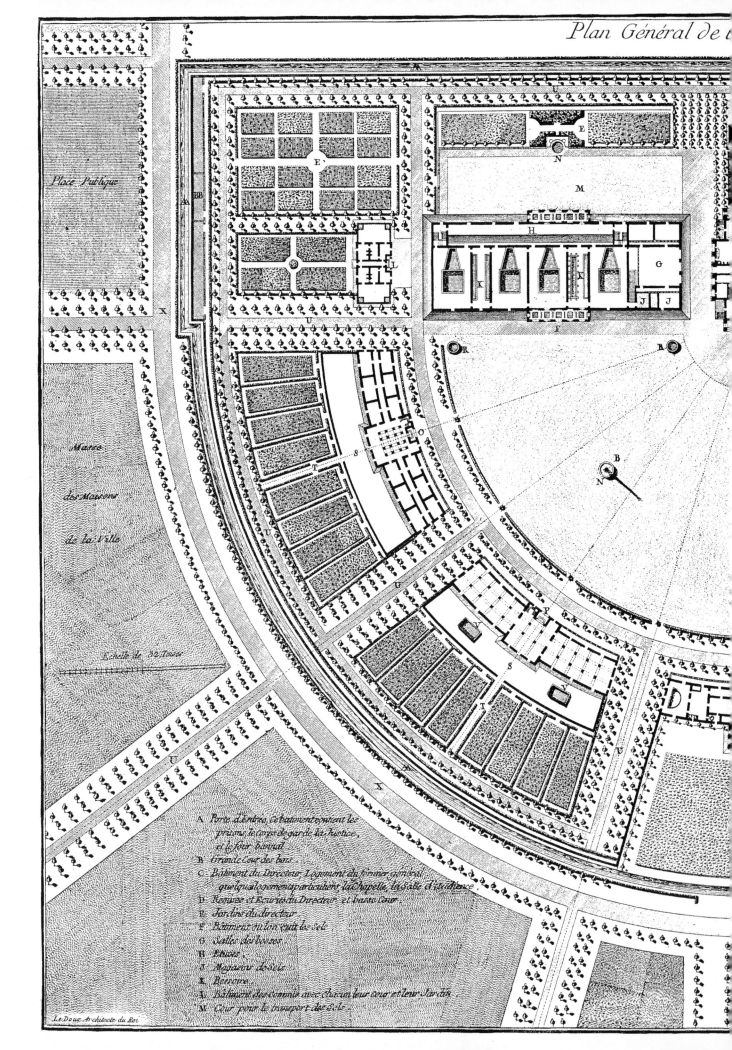

Plan of the existing buildings. The evaporation sheds flank the director's house and form the chord of the semicircle; the circumference is workers' housing and market gardens.

Place Publique

Masee des Maisons de la Ville

Echelle de 32 Toises

A Porte d'Entrée, ce batiment contient les prisons, le corps de gar de la Justice, et le four banal.

B Grande Cour des bois.

C Batiment du Directeur, Logement du fermier général quelques logemens particuliers, la chapelle, la salle d'audience.

D Remises et Ecuries du Directeur, et basse cour.

E Jardins du directeur.

F Batiment où l'on cuit le sel.

G Salles des bosses.

H Etuves.

J Magasins des sels.

K Bercerie.

L Batiment des commis avec chacun leur cour et leur Jardin.

M Cour pour le transport des sels.

Le Doux Architecte du Roi.

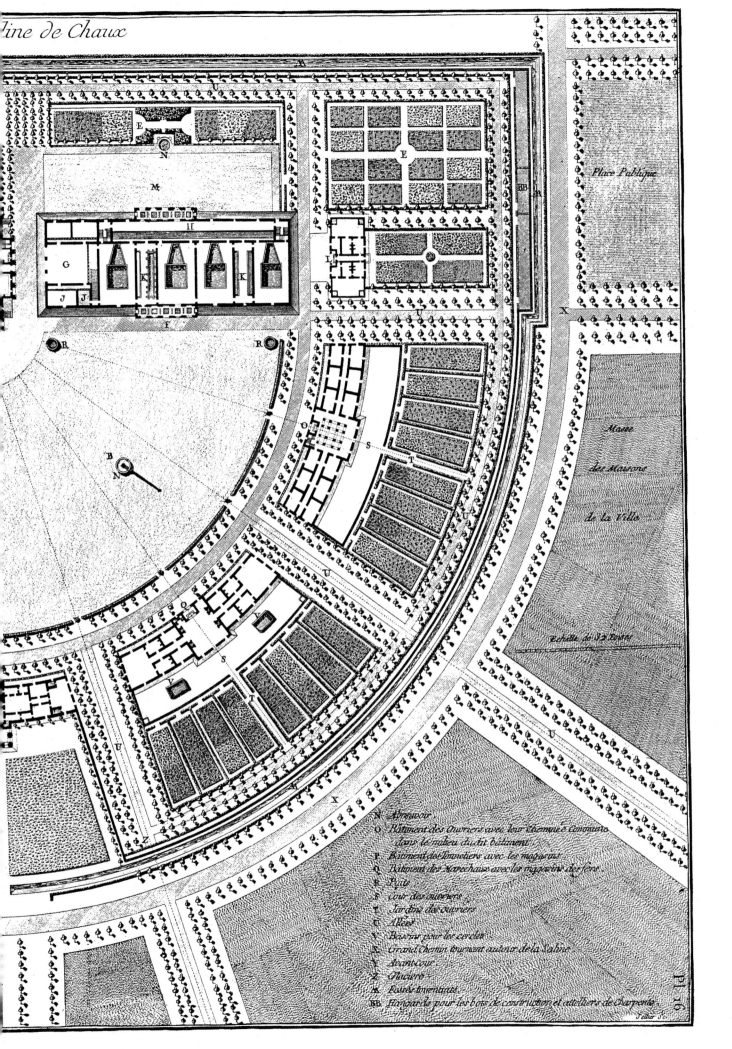

Place Publique

Masse

des Maisons

de la Ville

Echelle de 3 à Toises

N *Abreuvoir*
O *Bâtiment des Ouvriers avec leur chenupe é comquiste*
  dans le milieu dudit bâtiment
P *Bâtiment des Tonneliers avec les magasins*
Q *Bâtiment des Marechaux avec les magasins de fers*
R *Puits*
S *Cour des ouvriers*
T *Jardins des ouvriers*
U *Allées*
X *Bassins pour les cercles*
Y *Grand Chemin tournant autour de la Saline*
Z *Avant cour*
& *Glacière*
AA *Fossés tournants*
BB *Hangars pour les bois de construction et attelliers de Charpente*

Pl. 16

PALLADIO'S INFLUENCE   145

One of the evaporation sheds (left). The use of rustication and the alternation of arched and squared openings owes much to Palladio and his contemporaries.

A detail (above) of the central arch of the director's former coach house, today the garage for the director of the Center of the Future.

At the workmens' houses, the actual dwellings are in the lower buildings; the central building is a communal chamber. The main ornamental venture is seen, in the flanking wings, in the sculptured jars pouring solidifying liquid – a reference to the main business of the settlement, which was the evaporating of saline waters into kitchen salt.

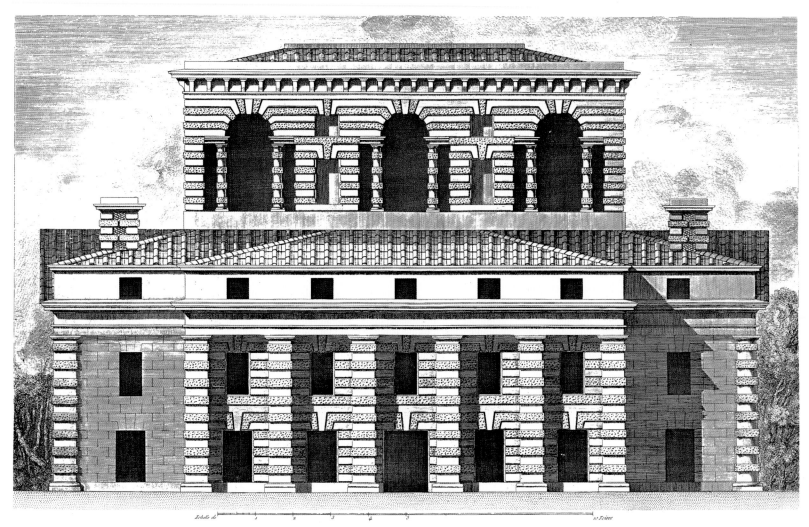

Elévation du Batiment de la direction sur le Côté.

The projected director's house:
elevation (above) and longitudinal
section (facing page) showing
the tall attic and section of the
central chamber, as well as a
chapel which was to be the nerve-
center of the settlement.

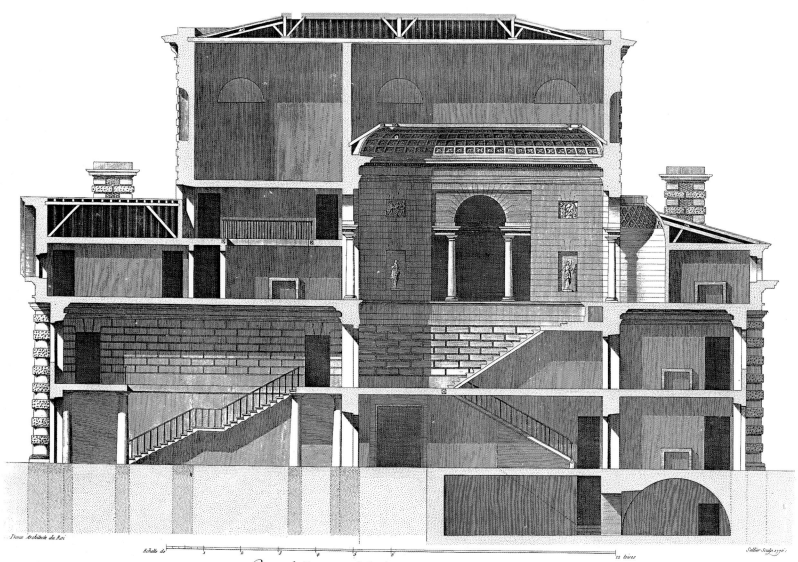

Coupe du Batiment de la direction Prise sur la Longueur.

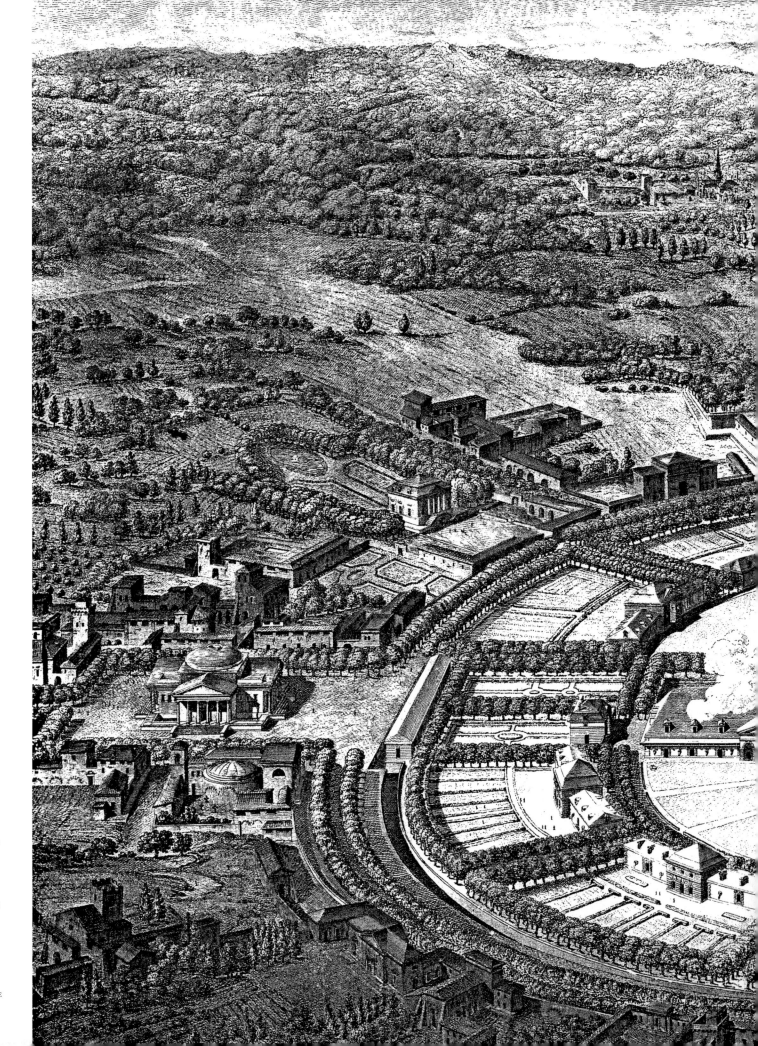

In Ledoux's plan for the settlement, the hemicycle is completed, however, only half was built; beyond, in the plan, are a number of ancillary and institutional buildings, all of which were individually designed to form the prototype of a "modern" town.

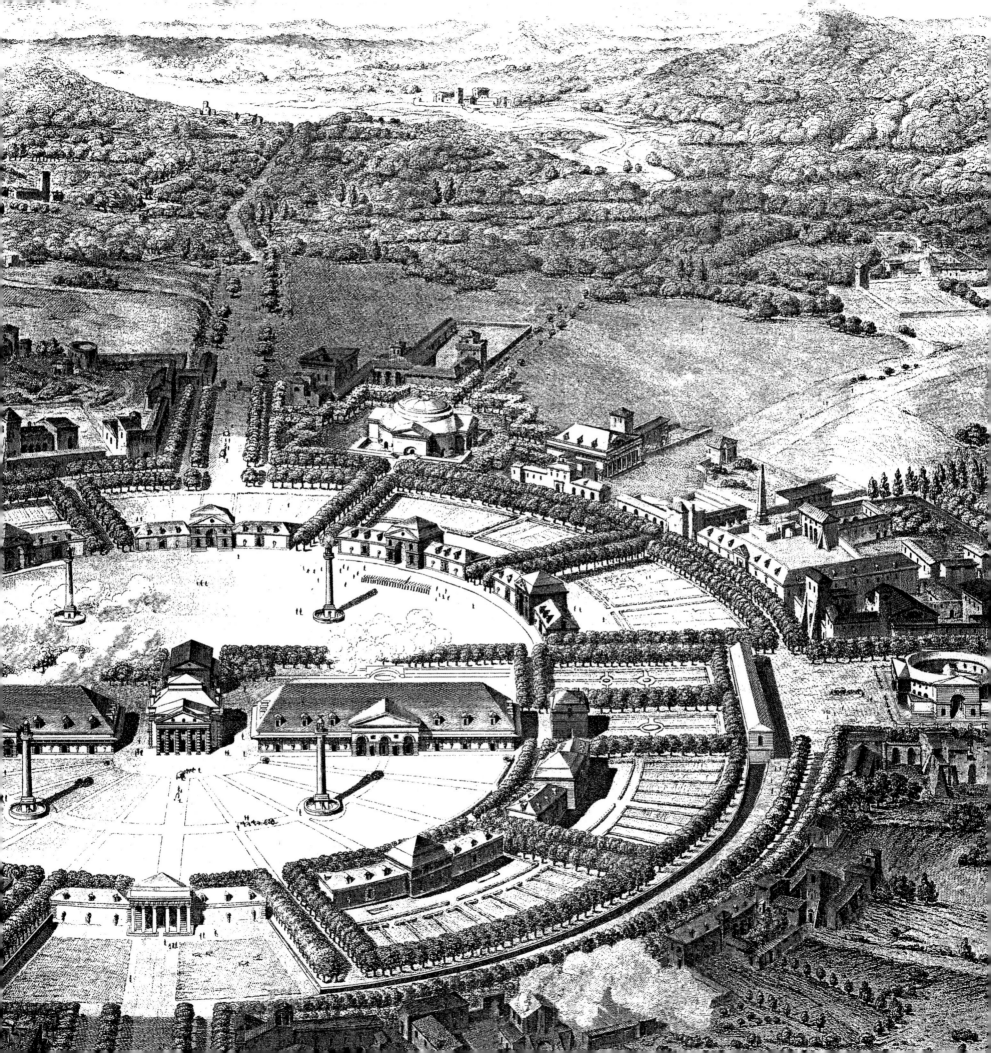

CHÂTEAU MONCLEY

Besançon

Château Moncley was designed by the architect Claude-Joseph-Alexandre Bertrand for the leading lawyer of the district, the first president of the newly-constituted *Parlement* (in fact, a law-court) of the Franche-Comté, of which Besançon is the capital. The lawyer was created Marquis de Terrier-Santans by Louis XVI about 1780. Bertrand, who had already built a town house for Santans in Besançon, also collaborated with Ledoux on the theater of the town and designed the houses surrounding it, as well as the church of Saint Pierre and the Fontaine des Dames in Besançon. He began work on Moncley, for Santans, just before the Revolution, but further building continued after 1830. Although the château retains a neo-classical appearance, large sections of it, and in particular the grand vestibule and the chapel, date from the early twentieth-century when it was acquired by Count de Lagarde. The proportions of the main salons, however, have remained unaltered, as has the semicircular courtyard.

The garden front's circular salon illustrates a feature used by several architects in the late eighteenth century.

Overleaf: The principal facade of the château.

The main hall, looking down to the entry from the monumental staircase (above).

The main hall, looking toward the monumental staircase from the entry (facing page).

Overleaf: A lateral wall in the main entry.

CHÂTEAU DE TANLAY

Tanlay

ALTHOUGH THE Château of Tanlay dates from medieval times, its first great period of building was when it belonged to the leading protestant family, the de Coligny, who in the seventeenth century made Tanlay a Huguenot center. A brother of the great Admiral de Coligny, who also resided there, François D'Andelot, carried out much of the work. His granddaughter sold Tanlay to a Lyons banker (of Italian origin) and royal functionary, Michel Particelli (who was allowed to add the title Seigneur d'Hémery, connected to Tanlay, to his name). After 1643, he employed the very prolific Pierre Le Muet (1591–1669), the translator of parts of Palladio's treatise into French (as a handbook to the use of the orders), who had been named *architecte du Roy*. He made frequent free use of columns rising several stories, as here at Tanlay, particularly on the garden facade. During Particelli's time much of the present splendor was added to the château—the stately entrance and the extensive water gardens. It is fortunate that Tanlay escaped the destruction that followed the Revolution—since the lords of Tanlay were resident landlords on good terms with their tenants.

As in most French châteaux, as at Anet, the medieval square layout is taken up by the layout of the modern building; the main square court is bounded by an imposing block which contains the main reception rooms, the *corps de logis*, on either side of which the lower wings contain the subsidiary accommodation. At the joint between wings and main block are the domed, octagonal towers that were done under the de Colignys, as was the outer gateway or entrance pavilion, which was finished in 1575.

At the main approach, the rusticated obelisks that guard the bridge over the moat echo the rustication of the triumphal gate, which is the inner gateway of the building. Its rather forbidding, rusticated and practically windowless lower story is surmounted by a sturdy, but pilastered and openly windowed upper floor and a steeply pitched roof. Parts of the main buildings were resurfaced, from 1643 to 1649, by Le Muet, who also designed the main entry gate with its heavily ringed Doric columns.

The main building, entirely
surrounded by a moat, is entered
by a bridge leading to the entry
gate designed by Le Muet in
the seventeenth century.

This wall encloses a small dependent château (not shown) just outside the main entry of Tanlay.

In the grand gallery, trompe-l'oeil frescoes in grisaille on ceiling and walls imitate architectural detail and sculptures. This rather grand chamber was shortened and the frescoes repainted after a fire in the late eighteenth century.

Details of the painting in grisaille
by Italian artists in the grand
gallery on the ground floor,
added by Le Muet after 1643.

In the corner tower, called the
League Tower, in reference to the
mid-sixteenth-century Wars of
Religion, the painted inner dome
has improbably been attributed
to Francesco Primaticcio,
and allegedly shows the main
personages of the Protestant
and the Catholic parties at the
court as the gods of Olympus.

Details from the paintings of the League Tower represent Pallas Athena (right), double-faced Janus (below – perhaps a caricature of the king who will not make up his mind between the parties), and the forge of Vulcan (facing page).

WILTON HOUSE

Wiltshire

WILTON HOUSE, designed by Isaac de Caus with Inigo Jones, was begun in 1636, and rebuilt after a fire in 1647 for Philip, fourth Earl of Pembroke. There had been a nunnery on the site and when the monasteries were abolished by Henry VIII, he gave the Abbey and the land to William Herbert (a brother-in-law of his last wife, Catherine Parr), whom he created Earl of Pembroke. Philip, his grandson, was further enriched by the gift of Trinidad, Tobago and Barbados from James I, though he later turned against Charles I and served the Commonwealth. The rebuilding of Wilton House in his time is not clearly documented. Isaac de Caus (or de Caux) had begun his career as a garden designer, working with his father Solomon, though John Aubrey in his *Lives* calls him "an ingeniouse architect." He remained in England and worked often with Inigo Jones. At Wilton he seems to have been both the executant architect and the garden designer. When parts of the house burnt in 1647/48, the rebuilding was carried out by John Webb, a kinsman and collaborator of Inigo Jones. The traditional association with Jones therefore seems substantiated.

At the south, garden front, a Palladian window (or *serliana*) is in the center; the raised corner pavilions may owe something to Serlio, or yet echo the corner towers Palladio sometimes used, as at the Villa Pisani in Lonigo (p. 62).

Overleaf: The "Palladian" bridge of 1737 at Wilton House, which runs over the River Nadder, was built by Roger Morris and the (ninth) Earl of Pembroke. The bridge is based on a drawing by Palladio, and was imitated elsewhere in England.

In the celebrated Double Cube
room, which is 60 by 30 by 30
feet, the decoration, perhaps
more French than Italian in
inspiration, is original and was
designed to accommodate (as
it still does) the family portraits
by Sir Anthony van Dyck.

A detail (right) of the eighteenth-century carved, gilded furniture in the Double Cube room. The central ceiling panels in the Double Cube room (facing page) are of the legend of Perseus, painted by Emanuel de Critz. The surrounding decoration by Edward Pierce incorporates the Herbert (the family name of the Earls of Pembroke) motto, "I shall only serve one master."

At one end of the Double Cube room is the family portrait of the Herberts of Pembroke by van Dyck, painted in 1633–34. All of the later furniture in the room is by Thomas Chippendale and William Kent. The elaborately decorated interior, in contrast to the rather austere exterior, is typical of the work of Inigo Jones. The carved head (above) is in the corner of the room just under the gilded cove.

CHISWICK HOUSE

Middlesex

THE EARL OF BURLINGTON probably began the design of Chiswick House before 1725. It had been a part of Burlington property for some time and there was a Tudor-Jacobean house on the ground to which the new Villa was skillfully connected. It is a much more explicitly "correct" building, in its careful adaptation of Palladian themes via Scamozzi, than the more aggressive Mereworth Castle (p. 198), which must have been begun only months earlier. The two houses are quite clear programmatic statements against the prevailing taste associated with the old Office of Works (see p. 23) that had been dominated by Wren, Vanburgh and Hawksmoor.

For Chiswick House, Burlington chose the Corinthian order, reputedly copying the capitals of the Temple of Castor and Pollux in Rome; however, for the entablature he followed the more traditional system published by Palladio. Detail of porch corner, showing the Corinthian order.

Overleaf: The main, east front of Chiswick House, with its highly unorthodox double staircase, which more probably reflects Italian design of the time than English.

In the gallery (above), two gilt
pedestals by William Kent
stand in front of the "Palladian"
window.

In the passage linking the villa
with the old Tudor-Jacobean
house (above right), the square
central room is screened by
composite columns, and there
are flat relieving arches over the
cornice. The ceiling is copied
from an antique model.

In the octagonal dome over the
salon, or *tribuna* (facing page),
Burlington used segmental
mullioned windows like those in
Roman thermae.

In the corner circular room there is a fireplace after a design (for the Queen's House) by Inigo Jones (facing page).

The detail (top left) shows a decorative head above the fireplace that is mirrored across the room above a niche, while another detail (bottom left) is from the fireplace itself.

A view through the gallery to
the corner circular room
(facing page) with a detail of
the decorative fret in the apse
(above).

Overleaf: William Kent, with the
Earl of Burlington, laid out the
main vista of Chiswick House,
looking towards the exedra.

MEREWORTH CASTLE

Kent

COLEN CAMPBELL designed Mereworth Castle in Kent, about 1720, for Colonel the Honorable John Fane, who was to inherit the Earldom of Westmorland in 1736. He was an inveterate party goer and this, one of his several houses, was intended for entertaining local gentry as well as visitors to nearby Tunbridge Wells. As one of the very first buildings in the new Whig-Palladian manner (see p. 22), Mereworth harks back to Palladio's most emblematic project in the *Quattro Libri*, that of the Villa Rotonda, and takes the engraving as a model rather than the existing building. It even emulates the combination of stone for columns and dressings, stucco for wall surfaces, and keeps fairly close to the original, though the scale is enlarged. The curve of the dome is also steeper, and the lantern is blind, since the flues from twenty-four fireplaces are carried between the inner and outer skin of the dome and the lantern acts as their chimney. Mereworth also departs from its model in not being quite so intensely symmetrical; it is on a relatively flat piece of land and has not Malcontenta's splendid surrounding landscape. Of its castle antecedents, only the moat around the house remained, and it was filled in the nineteenth century.

Colen Campbell had been a protégé of Lord Burlington, but when, at the peak of his career in 1722, Campbell began the design of Mereworth Castle, which did not strictly follow the more restrained ideas of Burlington, Burlington dropped him in favor of William Kent.

The East Pavilion is one of two such structures. The architect is unknown, and the pavilions are later than the main house (of which they are much reduced versions), though a sketch by Campbell has been associated with them.

In the main circular salon under the dome, the stucco ornament was executed by Giovanni Bagutti to Campbell's designs (facing page).

The interior of the dome (above) shows only four, quite small openings.

Overleaf: The castle flanked by the East and West Pavilions.

PITZHANGER MANOR
Ealing, London

SIR JOHN SOANE, who designed Pitzhanger Manor from 1800 to 1803, was a rather sentimental person. He had imagined that his two sons would inherit his two passions: architecture and antiquities. He was also very attached to his teachers and predecessors. He bought, for instance, virtually all the drawings by the Adam Brothers that had remained in their office when it was sold. He had also been very attached to another architect of the earlier generation, George Dance (for whom he had worked). Dance, having fallen in love and married the daughter of the owner of Pitzhanger, had lived in the house, and had transformed some of it for his own use. Soane bought the old house and enlarged it (though he did not touch the rooms Dance had revised). He hoped Pitzhanger and its splendors would stimulate his sons, and that he and his wife could retire there. The interiors were extravagantly colored, with black, gold-veined marble dadoes, simulated porphyry and various polychrome schemes in the upper floors. As the sons grew up, it became increasingly clear that they would not inherit their father's passions, and indeed turned against him. His wife's health declined, and the house, attended to with such great hopes, was sold.

The front of Pitzhanger Manor takes up the triumphal arch arrangement Soane often used. The caryatids atop the columns are cast in artificial stone, as are the reliefs of the eagles below them.

The Ionic columns at the front of
Pitzhanger Manor (facing page)
flank the imperial eagles (above)
on the exterior.

The sunrise relief (after one
on the triumphal arch of
Constantine) is a cast of one by
Thomas Banks that Soane used
in the Bank of England.

Prinz-Karl-Palais

Munich

The Prinz Karl-Palais in Munich, of 1804–1806, was originally built by the architect Karl von Fischer for a French courtier, the Abbé Pierre de Salabert. It took its name from a brother of King Louis I, for whom the French painter-architect Jean-Baptiste Métivier transformed the palace after 1825. The prince lived there until 1875. It was about the last German Palladian building—with the gently rusticated wall between giant pilasters—before the onset of neoclassicism. Prinz-Karl-Palais has retained its character in spite of alterations in 1937 and in 1971, after which it became the office of the Bavarian premier.

Prinz-Karl-Palais is opposite the English Garden in Munich, at the beginning of the monumental Prinzregentenstrasse. Karl von Fischer began work on the palace when he was 21 years old, and still a student in Vienna at the Academy.

The main entrance to the palace, which is now the office of the Bavarian premier.

The capitals (above) of the stately Corinthian columns in the main hall of the palace (facing page) have more acanthus leaves than customary.

The exquisite pink and gold main salon (facing page) gives clear evidence why Prinz-Karl-Palais is considered the first mature example of classicist architecture in Munich. Classical reliefs (left) are at the center of the door panels.

Painted lunettes, this one with
martial ornament, are part of the
decorative motif of the cornice.

Corinthian pilasters surround the main salon, their capitals of white and gilded plaster flanked by swags of cornucopia.

Rotunda, University of Virginia

Charlottesville

Thomas Jefferson worked on the design and building of the University of Virginia and its main Rotunda in Charlottesville, Virginia, from 1817 to 1826. The campus enshrined some of his great educational visions. The rotunda at the head of it would house the repository of wisdom. From its porch you would look across the lawn down to the landscape beyond. On either side of the rotunda colonnades would be punctuated by the pavilions, which were to house the professors. Lecture rooms would be on the ground floors, so that students could walk through the colonnades between lectures while the professors—they would teach at home—would stay where they were. If there is one architect whose influence is evident in this project, it is Palladio of course, but Jefferson saw him through Ledoux-shaped spectacles. In his own house, Monticello, on a hill above Charlottesville, Jefferson again appealed to a Palladian precedent, the Villa Rotonda, but as it was transformed by Scamozzi and the English Palladians.

The interior of the Rotunda, the main focus of the campus, is surrounded by paired, composite columns painted white.

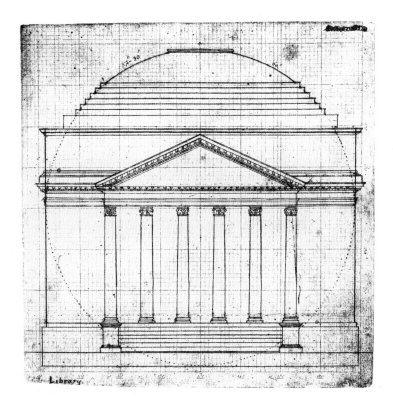

The front of the Rotunda is seen from the lawn – the open courtyard of the University campus.

In Jefferson's elevation (above) and section (below) drawings of the Rotunda, they, as many of his other drawings, are done on graph paper. This half-size "Pantheon" was intended as the Library of the University in the upper part, and is filled with oval committee rooms in the lower two floors.

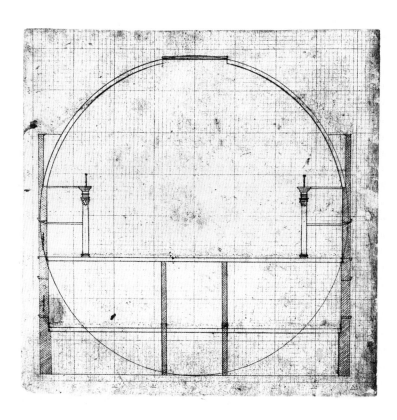

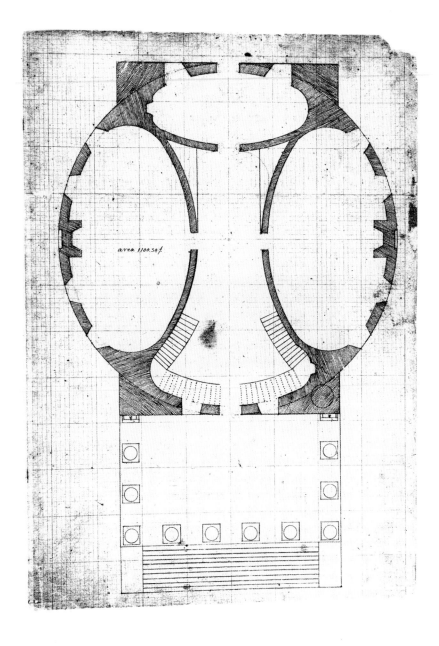

area 1100.50f.

Plan of the lower floors (above);
the staircase hall at the portico
level (facing page).

Overleaf: The interior of the
main, circular chamber of the
Rotunda is surrounded by paired,
composite columns.